the music glee

season 2 volume 6

R0061390860

12/2011

Series Artwork, Fox Trademarks and Logos
TM and © 2011 Twentieth Century Fox Film Corporation.
All Rights Reserved.

ISBN 978-1-4584-1214-0

HAL•LEONARD® CORPORATION

7777 W. BLUEMOUND RD. P.O.BOX 13819 MILWAUKEE, WI 53213

PALM BEACH COUNTY
LIBRARY SYSTEM
3650 Summit Boulevard
West Palm Beach, FL 33406-4198

For all works contained herein:
Unauthorized copying, arranging, adapting, recording, Internet posting, public performance,
or other distribution of the printed music in this publication is an infringement of copyright.
Infringers are liable under the law.

Visit Hal Leonard Online at
www.halleonard.com

TURNING TABLES

Words and Music by ADELE ADKINS
and RYAN TEDDER

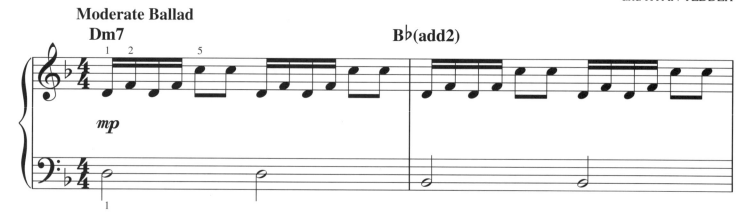

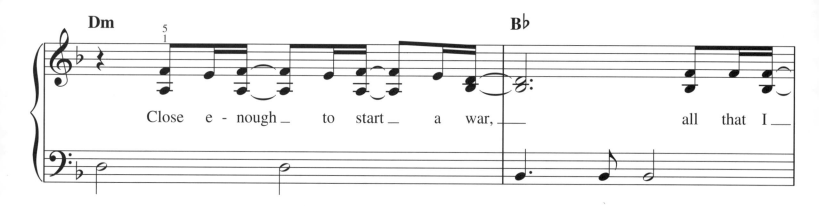

Close e - nough ___ to start ___ a war, ___ all that I ___

___ have _____ is on the floor.

Copyright © 2011 UNIVERSAL MUSIC PUBLISHING LTD. and WRITE 2 LIVE PUBLISHING
All Rights for UNIVERSAL MUSIC PUBLISHING LTD. in the U.S. and Canada Controlled and Administered by UNIVERSAL - SONGS OF POLYGRAM INTERNATIONAL, INC.
All Rights for WRITE 2 LIVE PUBLISHING Administered by KOBALT MUSIC PUBLISHING AMERICA, INC.
All Rights Reserved   Used by Permission

4

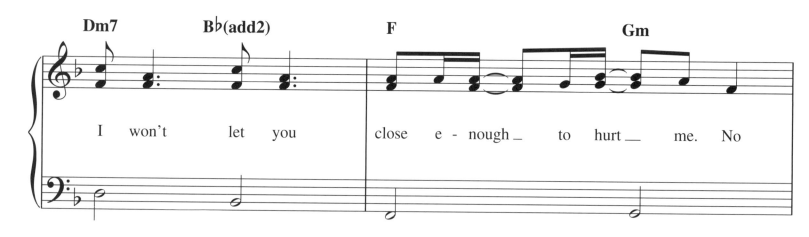

I won't let you close e-nough_ to hurt_ me. No

I won't res-cue you to just_ de-sert_ me. I can't

give you what you think_ you gave_ me._ It's time to

say good-bye_ to turn-ing ta-

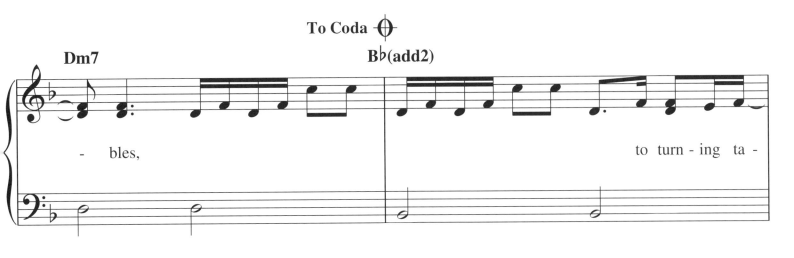

I braved a hun - dred storms _ to leave _ you, _____ as hard as you try, _

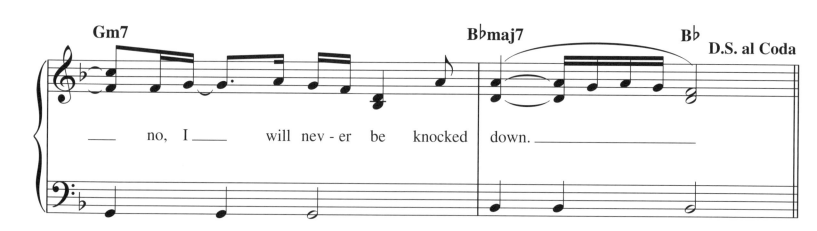

_ no, I ___ will nev - er be knocked down. _____

turn - ing ta - bles. _____

_____ Next time, I'll ___ be brav - er,

B♭maj7   **F**

I'll be my ___ own sav - ior when ___ the thun - der calls _ for me. _

Gm   **Dm**

_____ Next time, I'll ___ be brav - er,

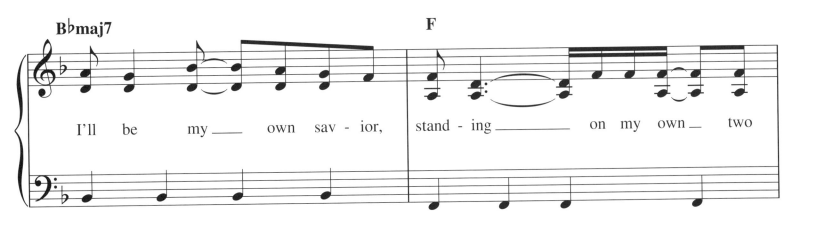

B♭maj7   **F**

I'll be my ___ own sav - ior, stand - ing _____ on my own _ two

C   **Dm7**   **B♭(add2)**

feet. _____ I won't let you

close e - nough _ to hurt _ me. No, I won't res - cue

you to just _ de - sert _ me. I can't give you

what you think _ you gave _ me. _ It's time to say good - bye _

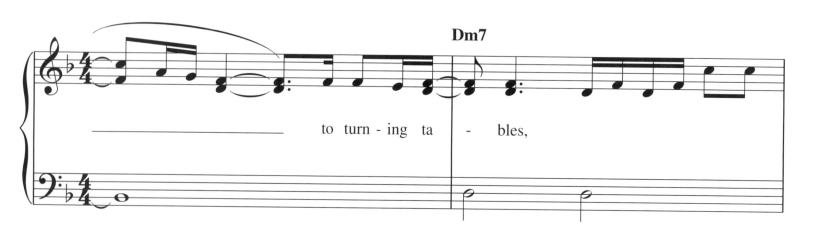

_ to turn - ing ta - bles,

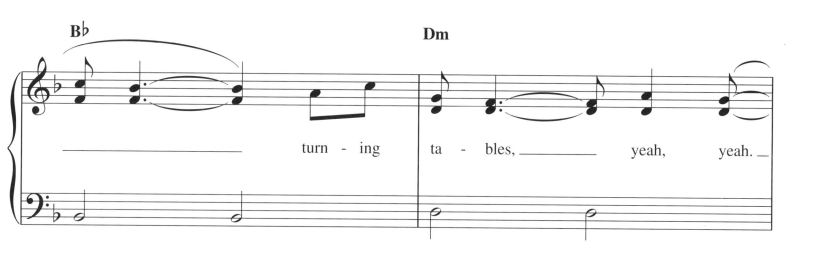

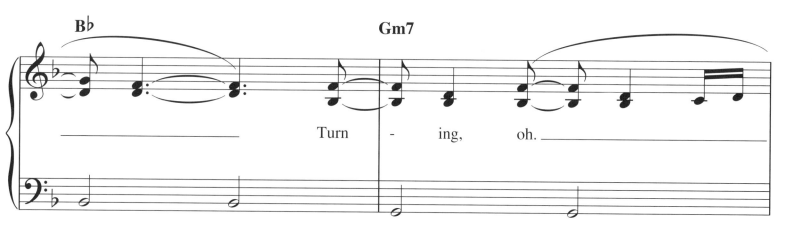

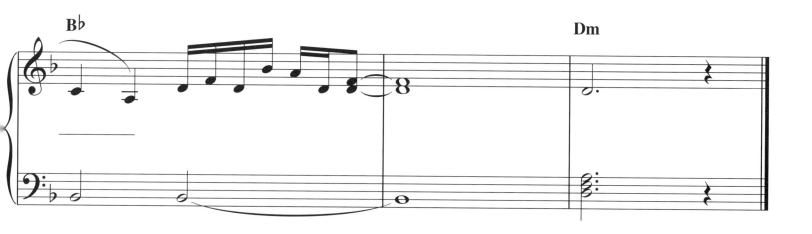

I FEEL PRETTY/UNPRETTY

Words and Music by DALLAS AUSTIN
and TIONNE WATKINS

© 1999 EMI BLACKWOOD MUSIC INC., CYPTRON MUSIC, EMI APRIL MUSIC INC. and GRUNGE GIRL MUSIC
All Rights for CYPTRON MUSIC Controlled and Administered by EMI BLACKWOOD MUSIC INC.
All Rights for GRUNGE GIRL MUSIC Controlled and Administered by EMI APRIL MUSIC INC.
All Rights Reserved   International Copyright Secured   Used by Permission

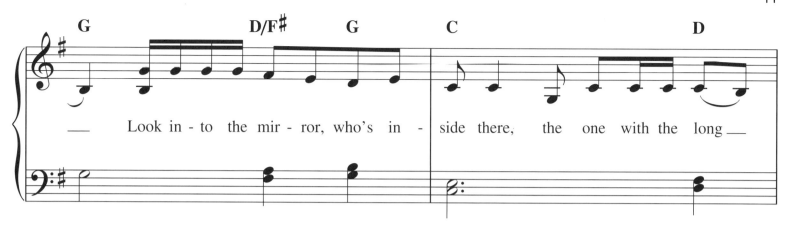

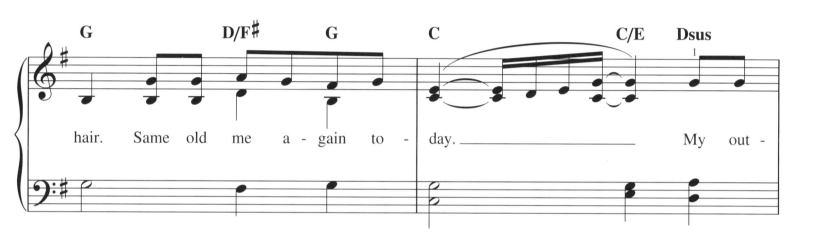

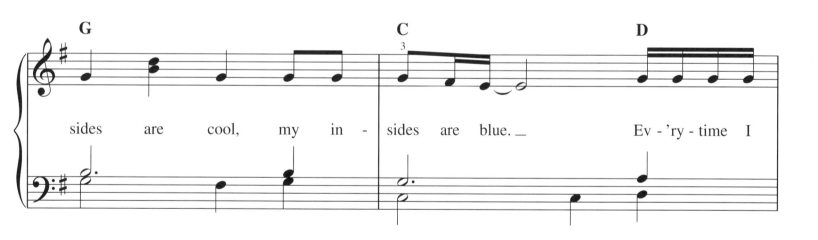

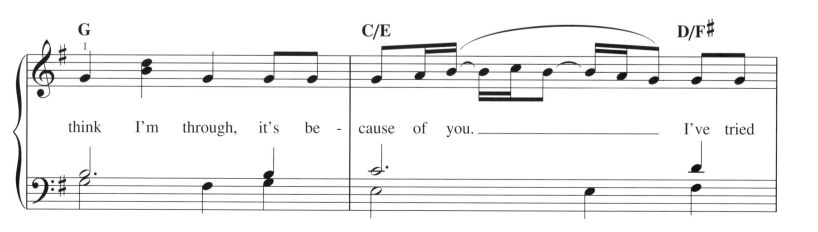

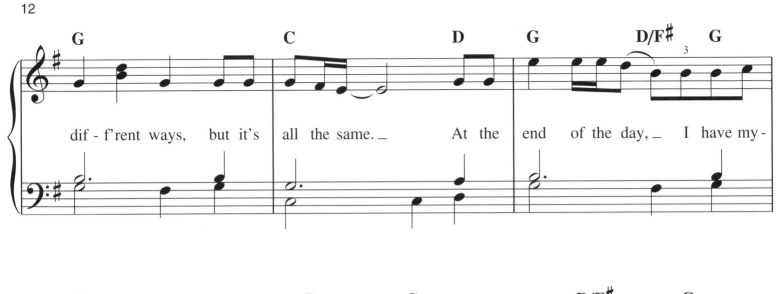

dif - f'rent ways, but it's all the same. ___ At the end of the day, ___ I have my-

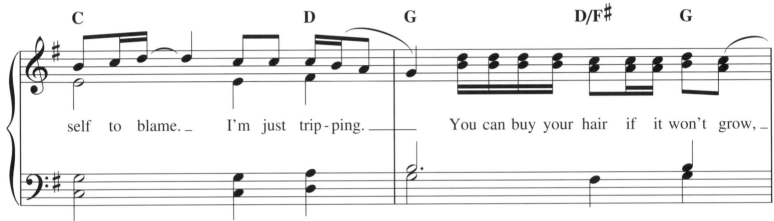

self to blame. ___ I'm just trip - ping. ___ You can buy your hair if it won't grow, ___

___ you can fix your nose if he says so. You can buy all the make - up that

MAC can make, ___ but if you can't look in - side you, ___

find out who I am, too. Be in a po-si-tion to make me

I FEEL PRETTY
from WEST SIDE STORY
Lyrics by STEPHEN SONDHEIM
Music by LEONARD BERNSTEIN

feel so damn un-pret-ty. I feel pret-ty, oh, so pret-ty. I feel

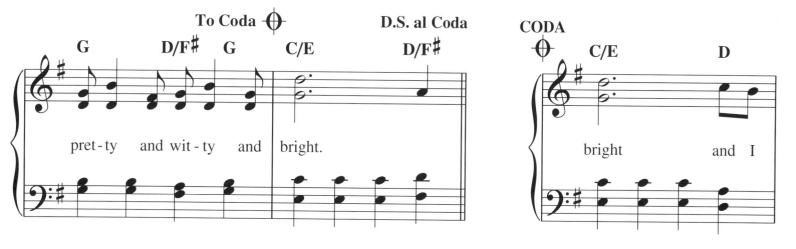

pret-ty and wit-ty and bright. bright and I

pit-y an-y girl who is-n't me to-night.

Copyright © 1957 by Amberson Holdings LLC and Stephen Sondheim
Copyright Renewed
Leonard Bernstein Music Publishing Company LLC, Publisher
Boosey & Hawkes, Inc., Sole Agent
Copyright For All Countries All Rights Reserved

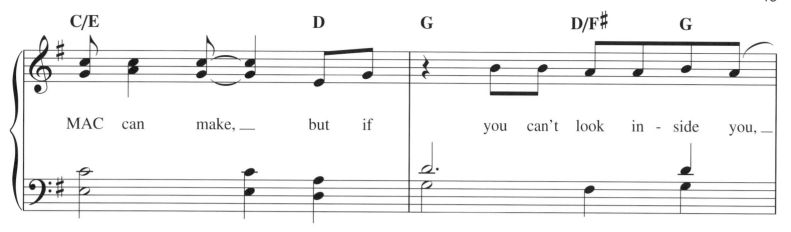

C/E MAC can make, ___ but if **D** **G** you can't look in - side you, ___ **D/F#** **G**

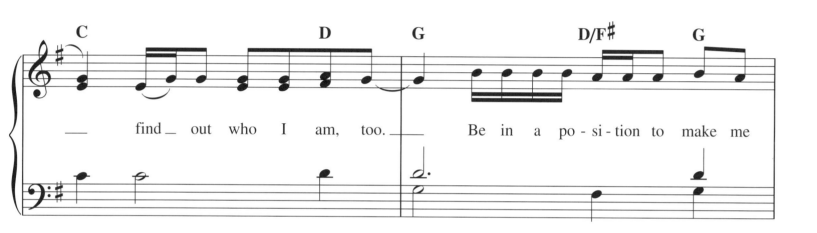

C ___ find ___ out who I am, too. ___ **D** **G** Be in a po - si - tion to make me **D/F#** **G**

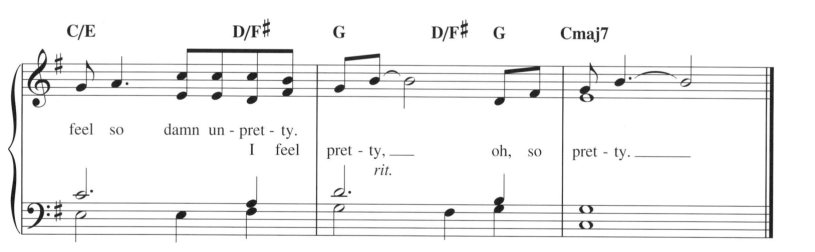

C/E feel so damn un - pret - ty. **D/F#** I feel **G** pret - ty, ___ *rit.* **D/F#** **G** oh, so **Cmaj7** pret - ty. _____

Additional Lyrics

Never insecure until I met you,
Now I'm being stupid.
I used to be so cute to me,
Just a little bit skinny.
Why do I look to all these things
To keep you happy?
Maybe get rid of you
And then I'll get back to me.

My outsides are cool...

AS IF WE NEVER SAID GOODBYE

from SUNSET BOULEVARD

Music by ANDREW LLOYD WEBBER
Lyrics by DON BLACK and CHRISTOPHER HAMPTON,
with contributions by AMY POWERS

© Copyright 1993 Andrew Lloyd Webber licensed to The Really Useful Group Ltd.
International Copyright Secured   All Rights Reserved

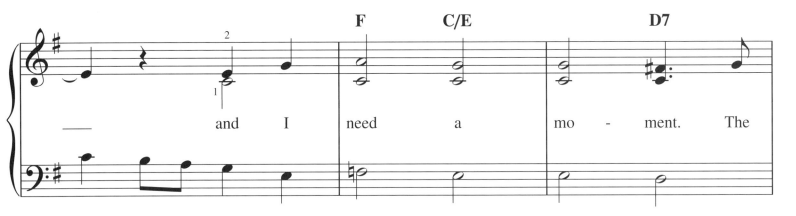

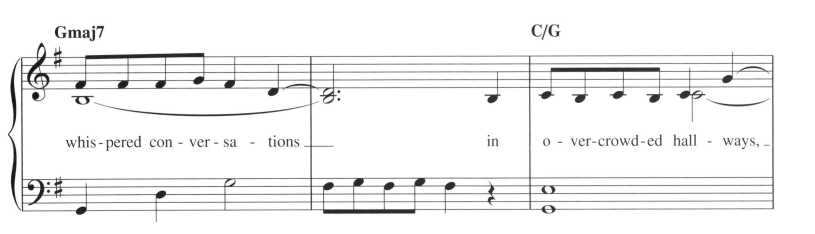

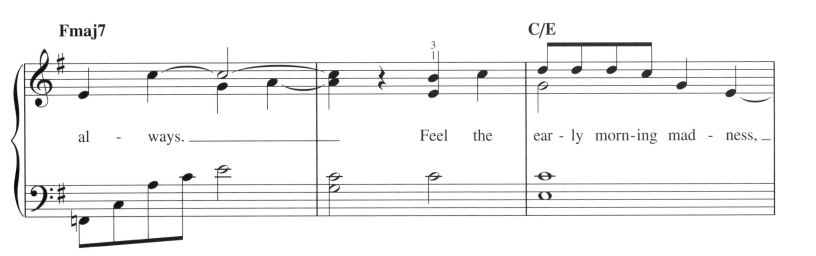

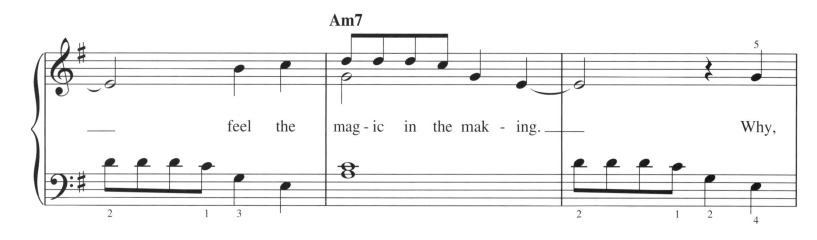

feel the mag - ic in the mak - ing. Why,

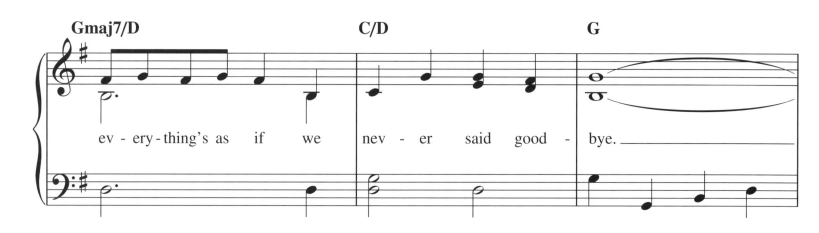

ev - ery - thing's as if we nev - er said good - bye.

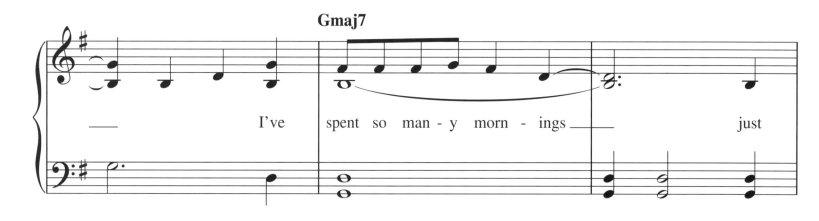

I've spent so man - y morn - ings just

try - ing to re - sist you, I'm trem - bling now, _ you

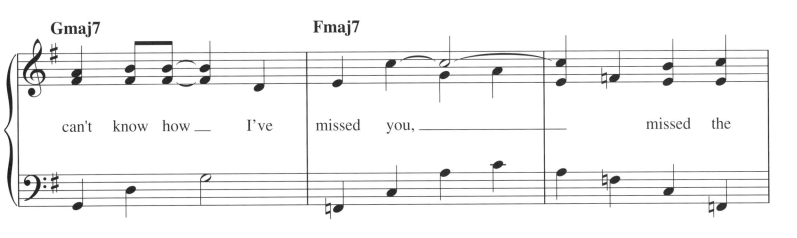

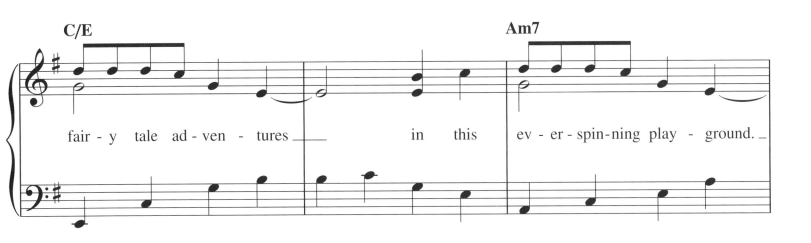

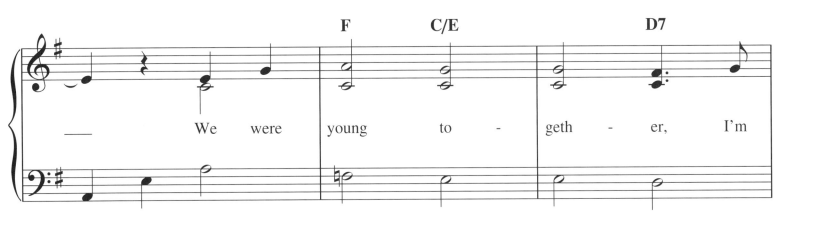

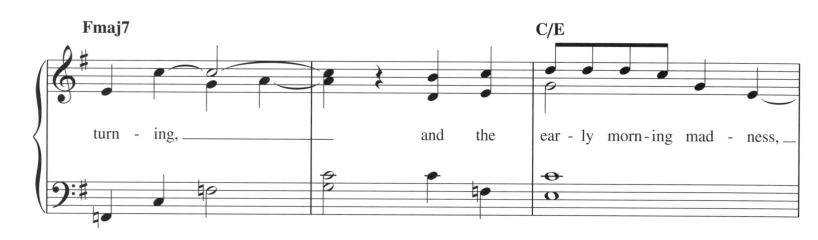

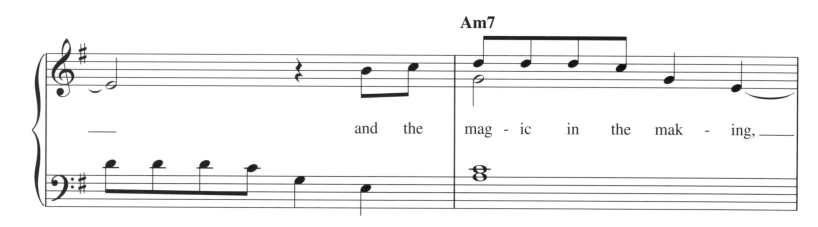

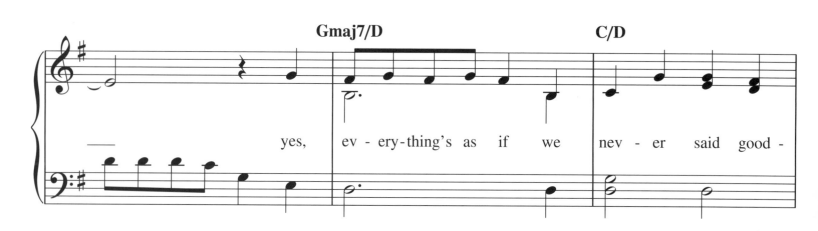

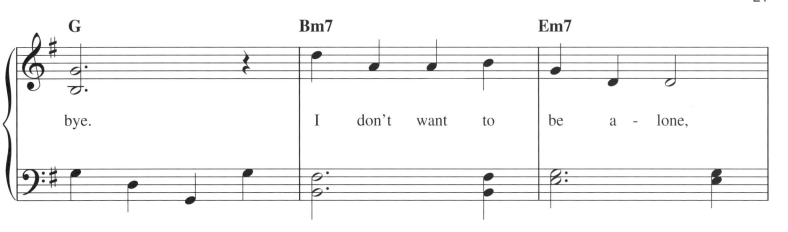

G   **Bm7**   **Em7**

bye.   I don't want to be a - lone,

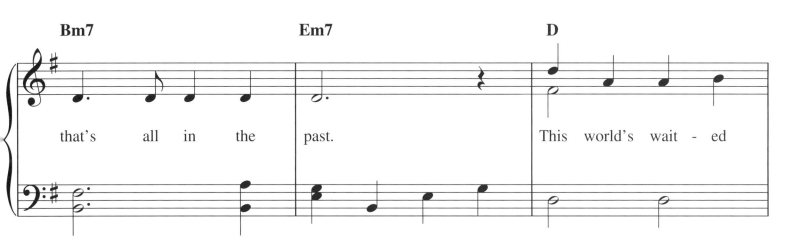

Bm7   **Em7**   **D**

that's all in the past.   This world's wait - ed

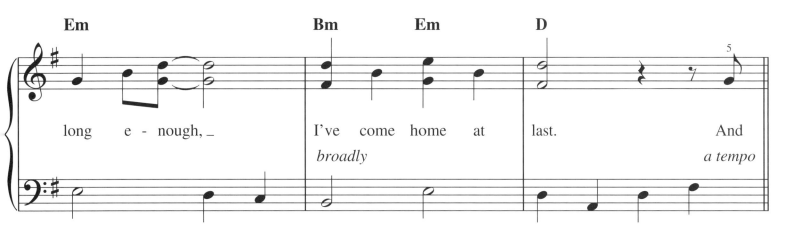

Em   **Bm**   **Em**   **D**

long e - nough, _   I've come home at last.   And

broadly   *a tempo*

Gmaj7   **C/G**

this time will be big - ger, __   and bright - er than we knew it, __

whis - pered con - ver - sa - tions __   in o - ver - crow - ded hall - ways, __

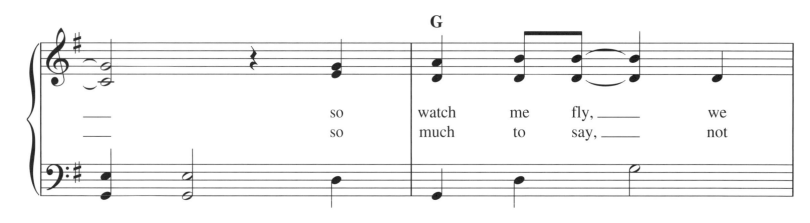

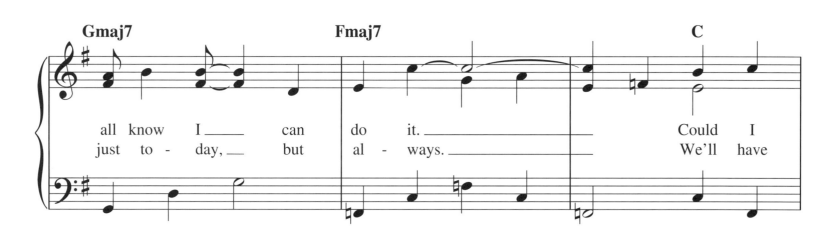

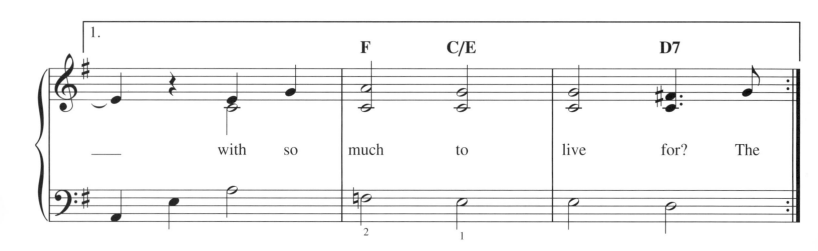

BORN THIS WAY

Words and Music by STEFANI GERMANOTTA,
JEPPE LAURSEN, PAUL BLAIR
and FERNANDO GARIBAY

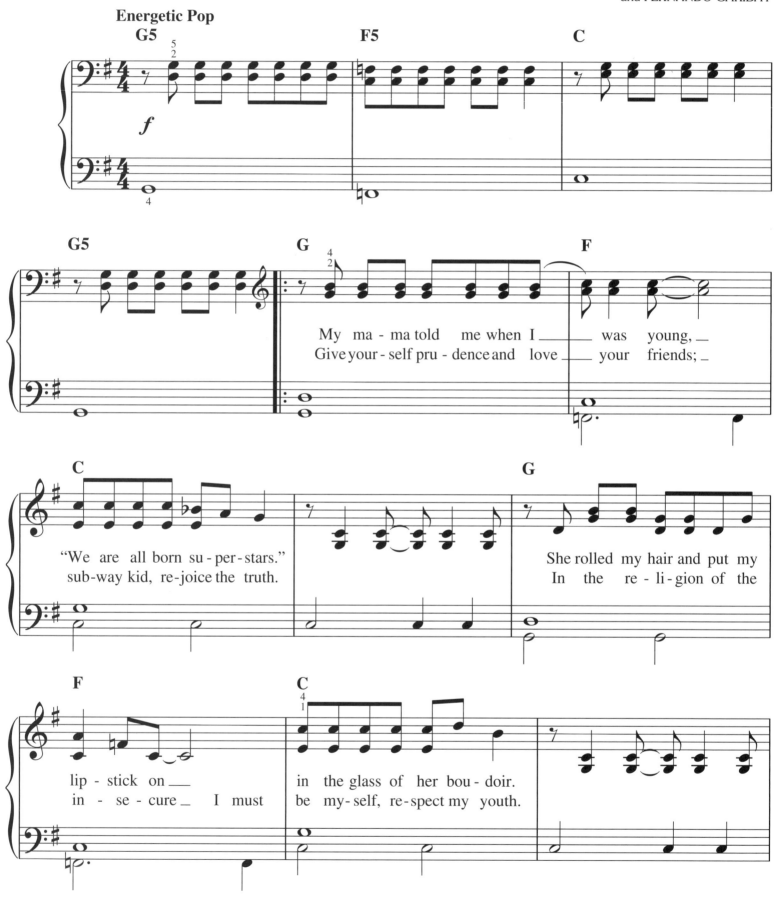

Copyright © 2011 Sony/ATV Music Publishing LLC, House Of Gaga Publishing Inc., Universal Music Corp., Warner-Tamerlane Publishing Corp. and Garibay Music Publishing
All Rights on behalf of Sony/ATV Music Publishing LLC and House Of Gaga Publishing Inc. Administered by Sony/ATV Music Publishing LLC, 8 Music Square West, Nashville, TN 37203
All Rights on behalf of Garibay Music Publishing Administered by Warner-Tamerlane Publishing Corp.
International Copyright Secured   All Rights Reserved

* *Mi amore vole fè* is an Italian phrase that means "My love needs faith."

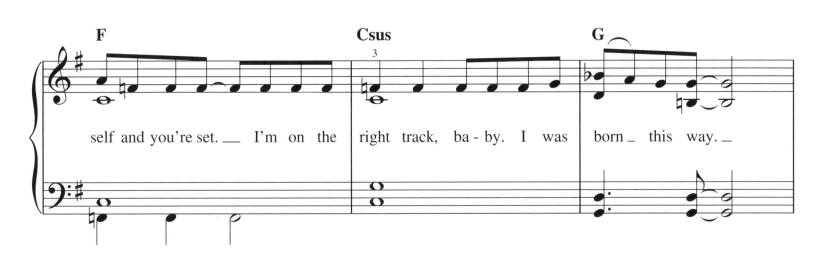

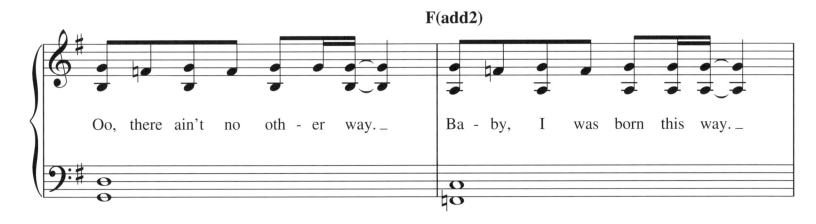

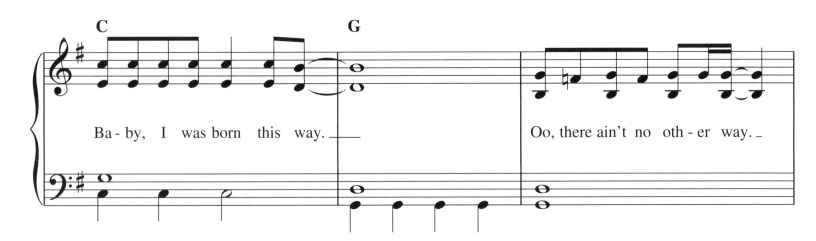

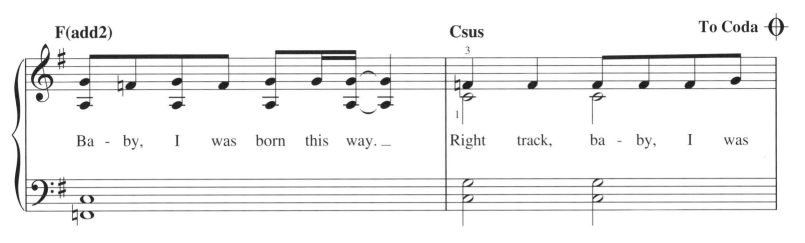

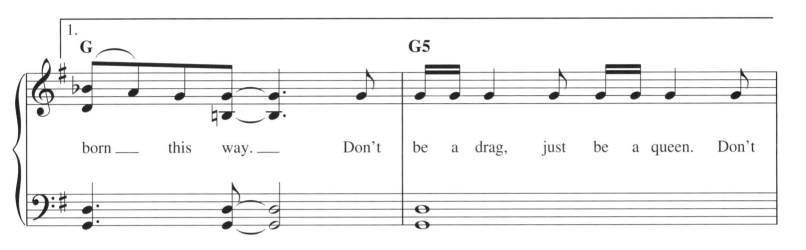

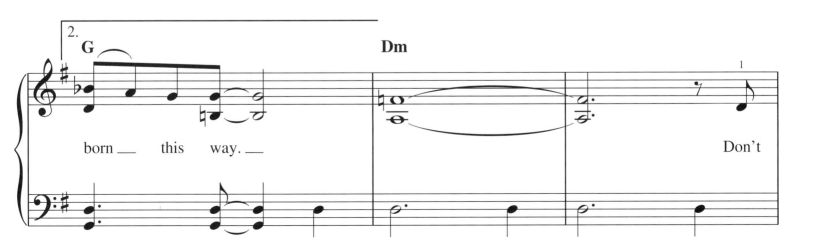

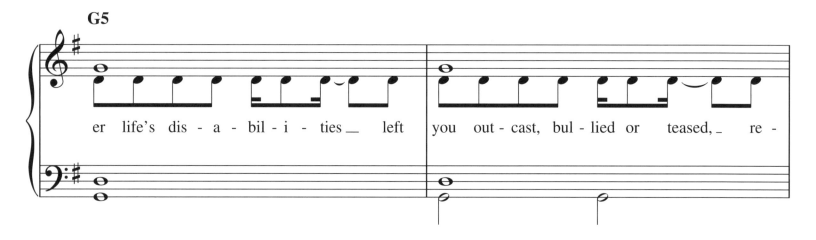

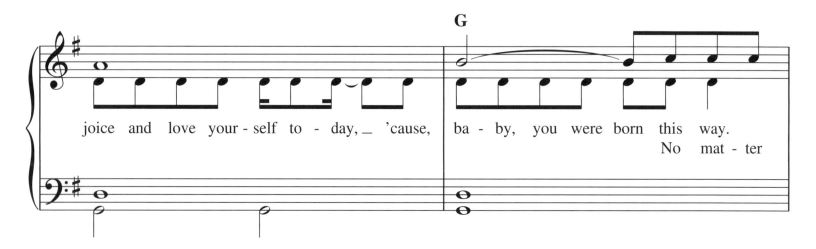

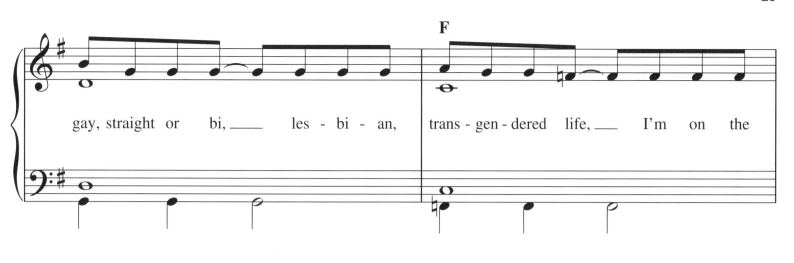

gay, straight or bi, ___ les - bi - an, trans - gen - dered life, ___ I'm on the

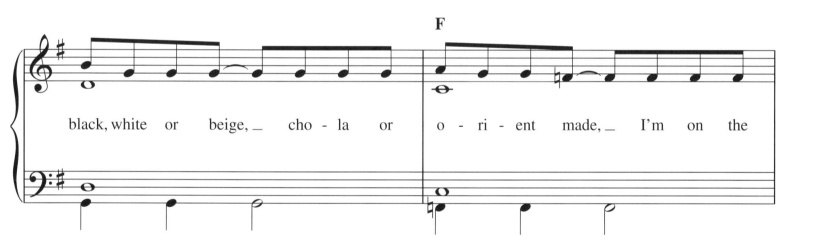

right track, ba - by. I was born to sur - vive. ___ No mat - ter

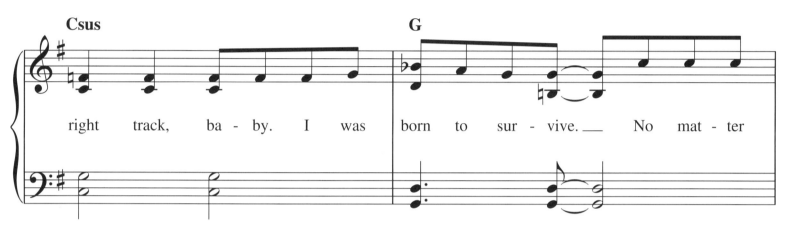

black, white or beige, _ cho - la or o - ri - ent made, _ I'm on the

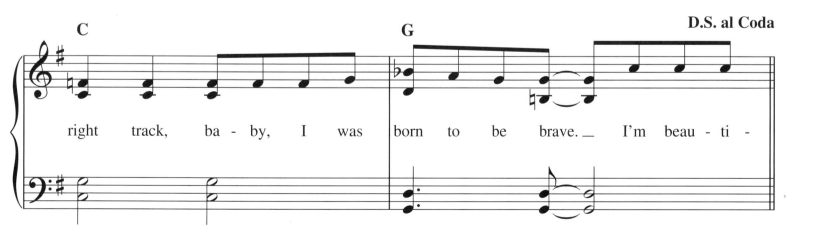

right track, ba - by, I was born to be brave. _ I'm beau - ti -

CODA

born _ this way. _ I was born this way, hey. _ I was

born this way, hey. _ I'm on the right track, ba - by. I was

born this way, hey. _ I was born this way, hey. _ I was

born this way, hey. _ I'm on the right track, ba - by. I was born this way, hey. _

DREAMS

Words and Music by
STEVIE NICKS

Now, here you go a - gain. __ You say
Now, here I go a - gain. __ I see

you want __ your free - dom.
the crys - tal vi - sions.

Well, who am I __
I keep my vi -

__ to keep __ you down? __
- sions to __ my - self. __

Copyright © 1977 Welsh Witch Music
Copyright Renewed
All Rights Administered by Sony/ATV Music Publishing LLC, 8 Music Square West, Nashville, TN 37203
International Copyright Secured   All Rights Reserved

It's on - ly right _____ that you _ should play the way _ you
It's on - ly me _____ who wants to wrap a - round your

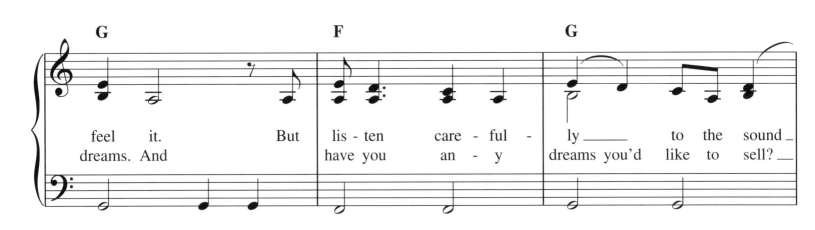

feel it. But lis - ten care - ful - ly _____ to the sound _
dreams. And have you an - y dreams you'd like to sell? _

_____ of your lone - li - ness, like a heart - beat, drives you mad, _
_____ Dreams of lone - li - ness, like a heart - beat, drives you mad, _

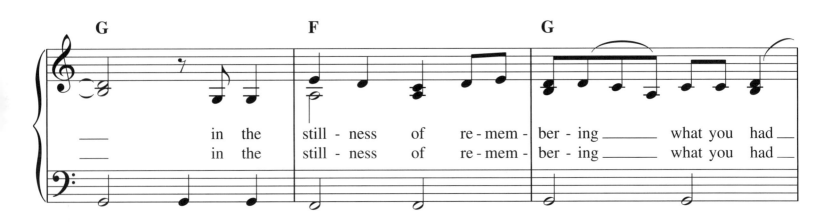

_____ in the still - ness of re - mem - ber - ing _____ what you had _
_____ in the still - ness of re - mem - ber - ing _____ what you had

and what you lost
and what you lost

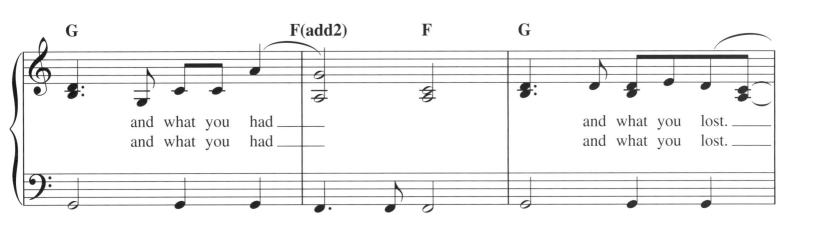

and what you had
and what you had

and what you lost.
and what you lost.

Oh, thun - der on - ly hap -

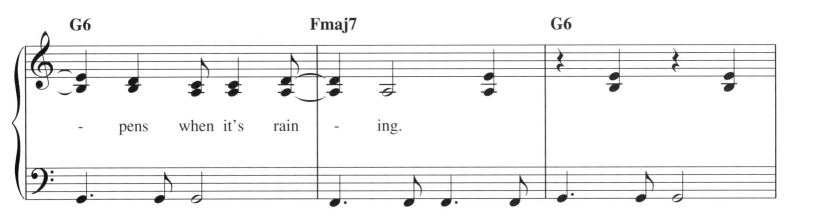

- pens when it's rain - ing.

Play - ers   on - ly   love   you   when they're play   -   ing. _____

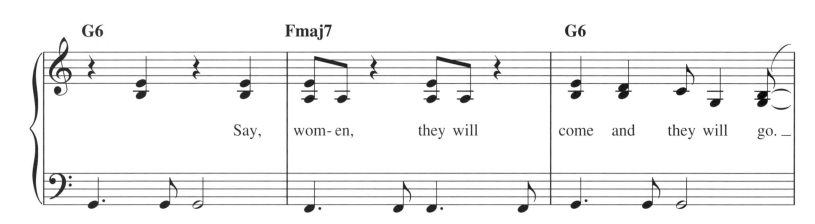

Say,   wom- en,   they will   come   and   they will   go. _

_____   When   the   rain wash - es _

To Coda ⊕

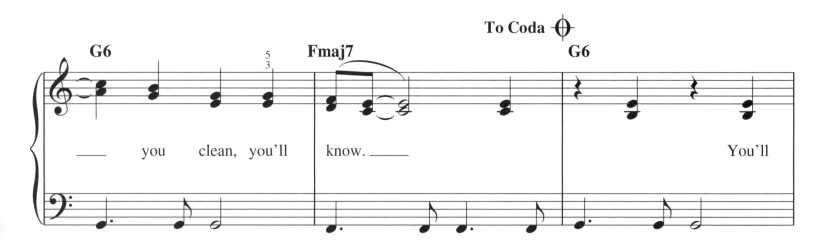

_ you   clean, you'll   know. _____   You'll

know. __

D.S. al Coda

You'll know __ You will

know. __ Oh, __ you'll know. __

rit.

SONGBIRD

Words and Music by
CHRISTINE McVIE

Copyright © 1977 by Universal Music - Careers
Copyright Renewed
International Copyright Secured   All Rights Reserved

the sun _____ will be shin - ing,
I'd nev - er be cold, _____
'cause I feel that when _ I'm

with you it's al - right. _____ I know _

_ it's right. _____ And the song - birds _____ keep

sing - ing like they know the score. _____ And I

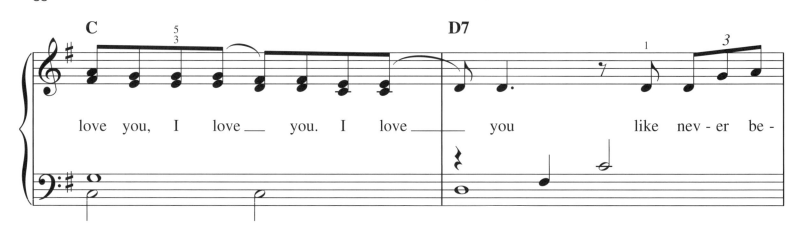

love you, I love ____ you. I love _____ you like nev - er be -

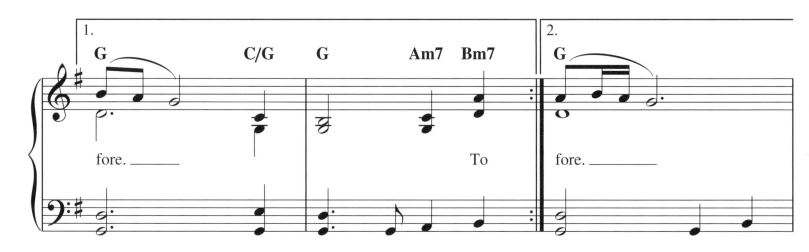

fore. _____ To fore. _____

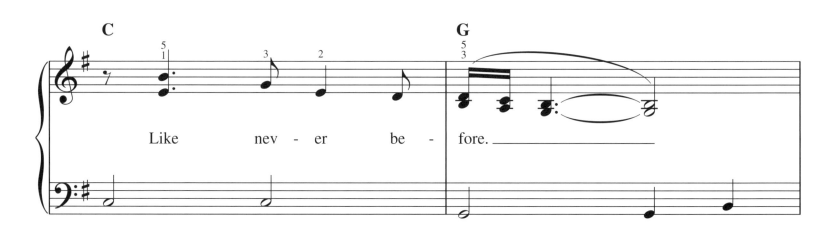

Like nev - er be - fore. _____

Like nev - er be - fore. ____ *rit.*

GO YOUR OWN WAY

Words and Music by
LINDSEY BUCKINGHAM

© 1976 (Renewed) NOW SOUNDS MUSIC
All Rights Reserved   Used by Permission

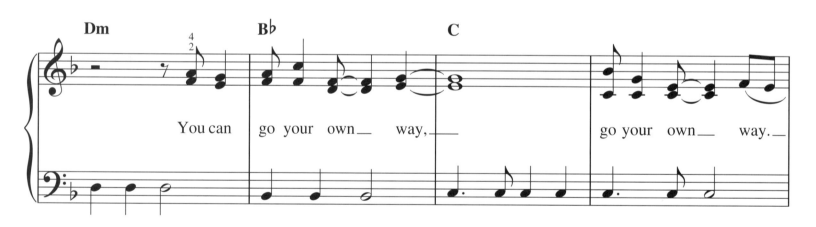

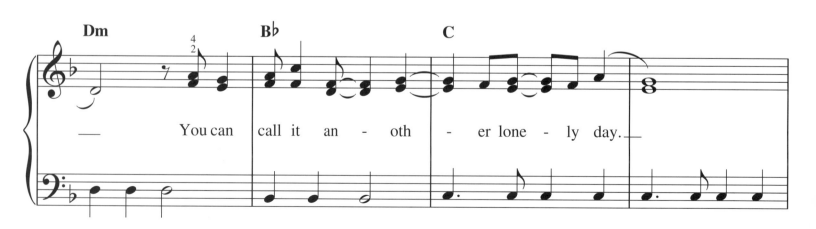

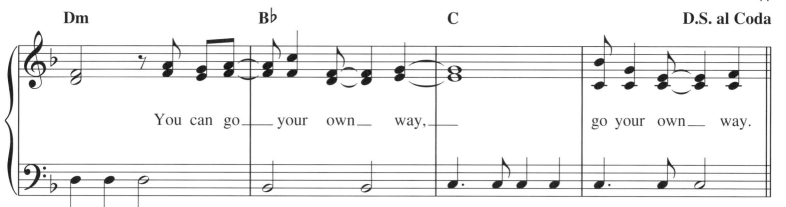

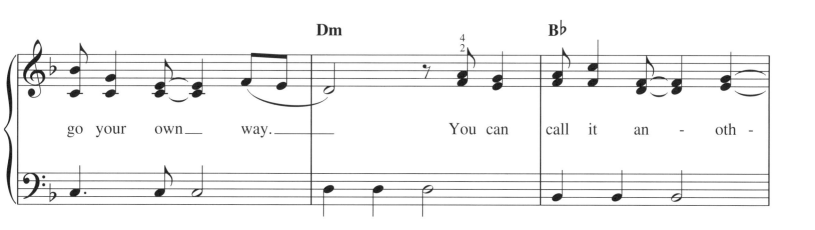

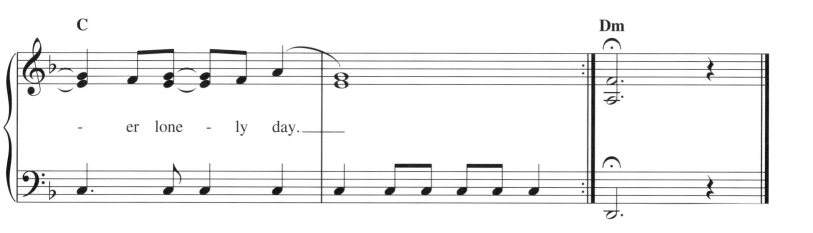

DON'T STOP

Words and Music by
CHRISTINE McVIE

Copyright © 1976 by Universal Music - Careers
Copyright Renewed
International Copyright Secured   All Rights Reserved

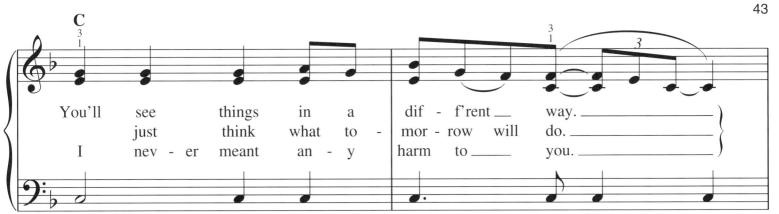

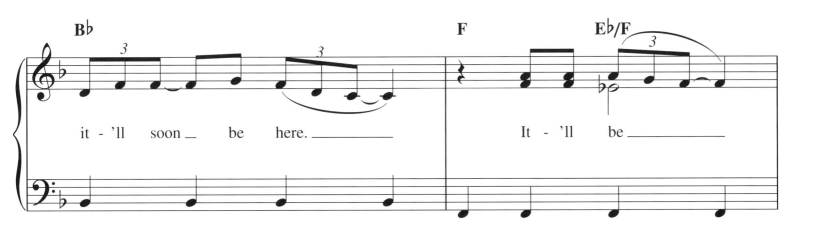

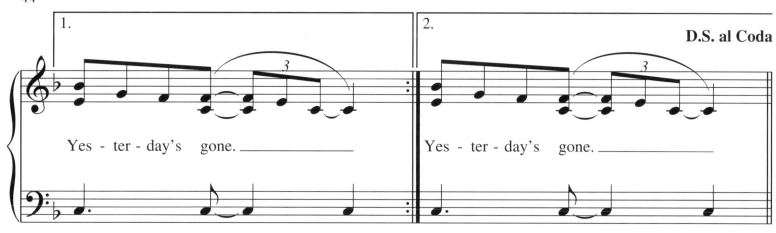

D.S. al Coda

Yes - ter - day's gone.

Yes - ter - day's gone.

CODA

Yes - ter - day's gone.

Oo,

don't you look back.

back.

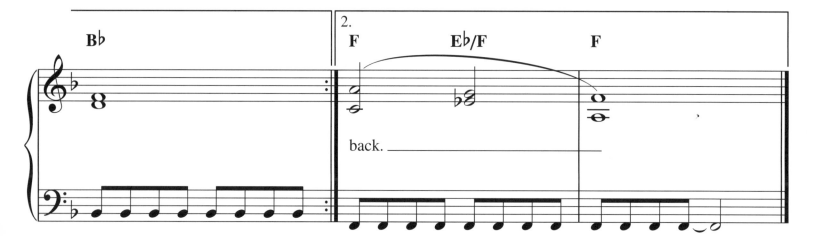

back.

ISN'T SHE LOVELY

Words and Music by
STEVIE WONDER

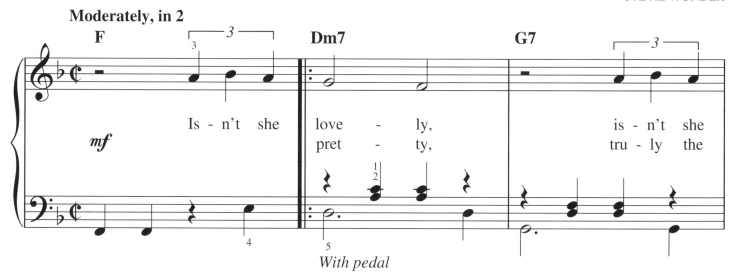

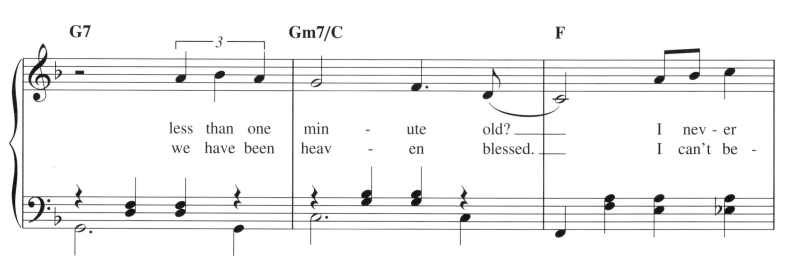

© 1976 (Renewed 2004) JOBETE MUSIC CO., INC. and BLACK BULL MUSIC
c/o EMI APRIL MUSIC INC.
All Rights Reserved   International Copyright Secured   Used by Permission

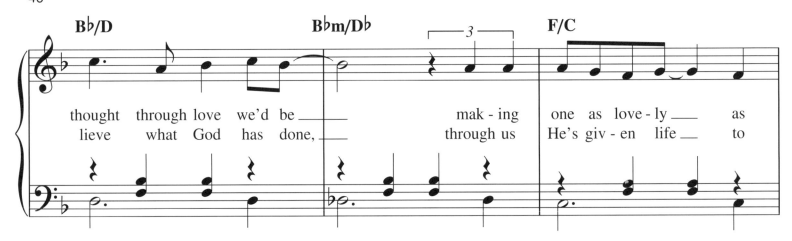

thought through love we'd be ___ mak-ing one as love-ly ___ as
lieve what God has done, ___ through us He's giv-en life ___ to

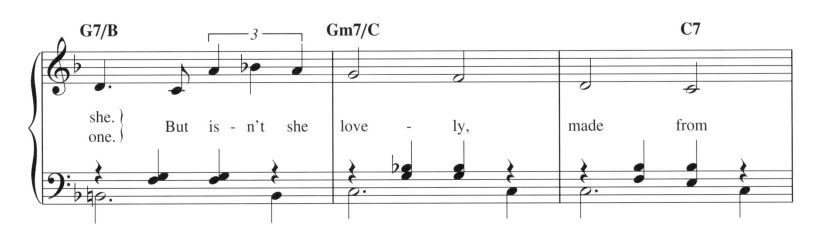

she. }
one. } But is - n't she   love - ly,   made   from

love?   Is - n't she   love - ly,

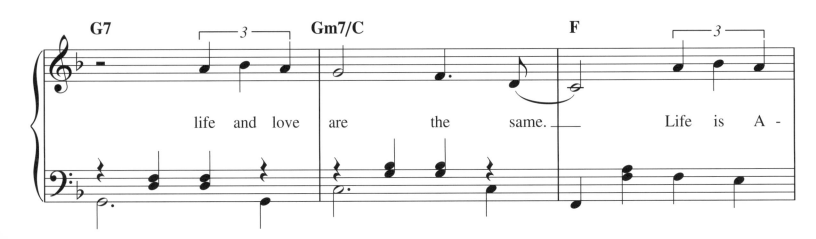

life and love   are   the   same. ___   Life is A -

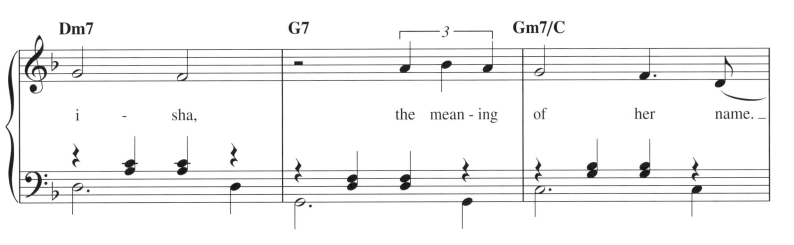

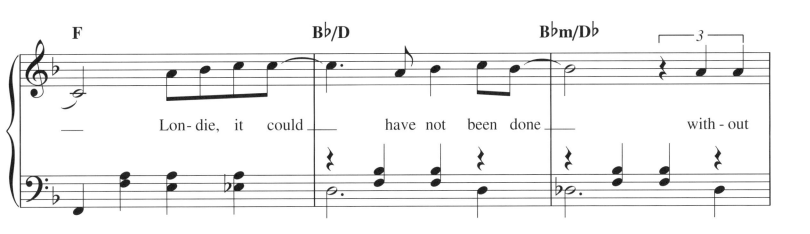

ROLLING IN THE DEEP

Words and Music by ADELE ADKINS
and PAUL EPWORTH

Copyright © 2010, 2011 UNIVERSAL MUSIC PUBLISHING LTD. and EMI MUSIC PUBLISHING LTD.
All Rights for UNIVERSAL MUSIC PUBLISHING LTD. in the U.S. and Canada Controlled and Administered by UNIVERSAL - SONGS OF POLYGRAM INTERNATIONAL, INC.
All Rights for EMI MUSIC PUBLISHING LTD. in the U.S. and Canada Controlled and Administered by EMI BLACKWOOD MUSIC INC.
All Rights Reserved   Used by Permission

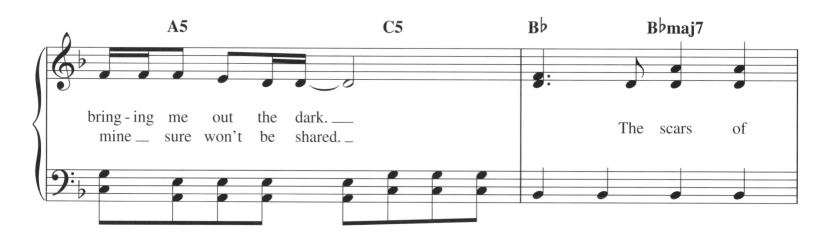

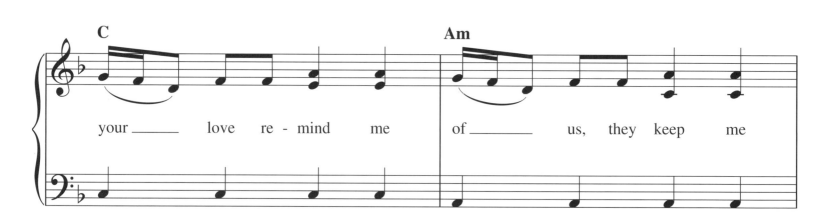

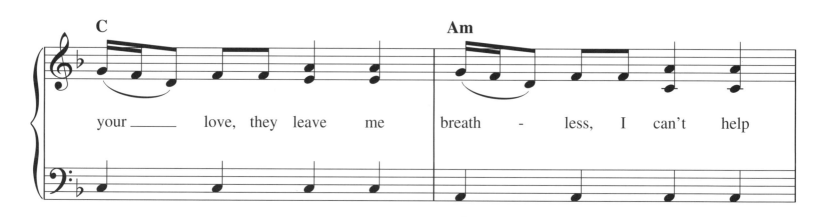

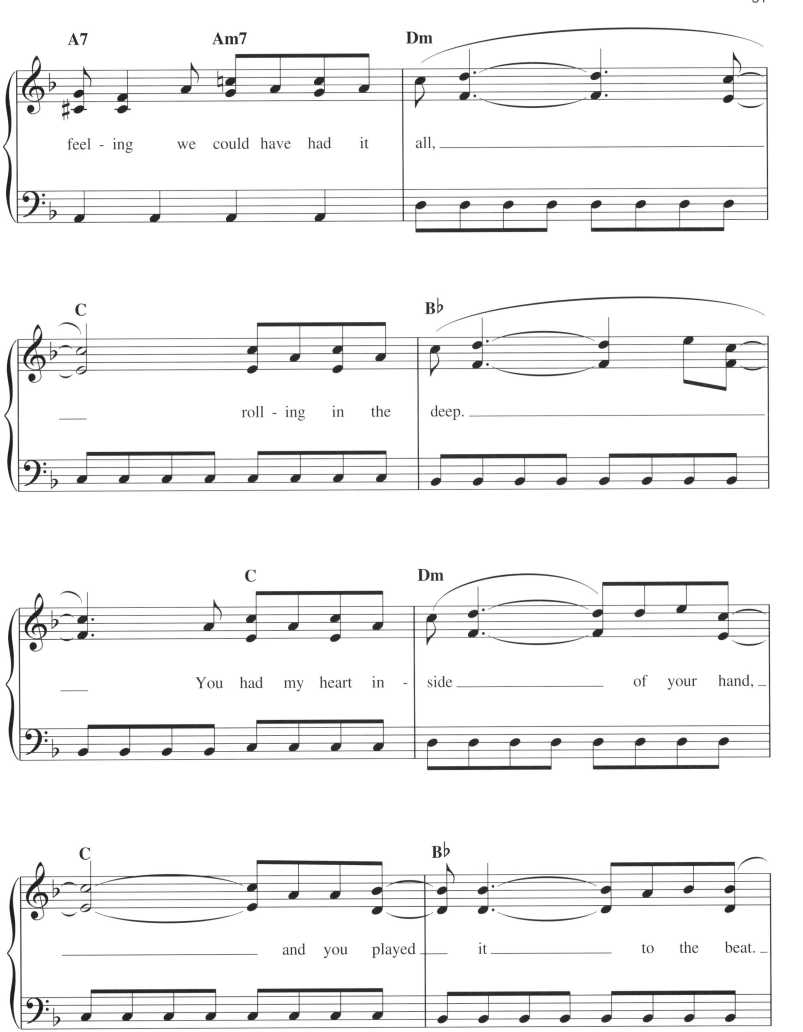

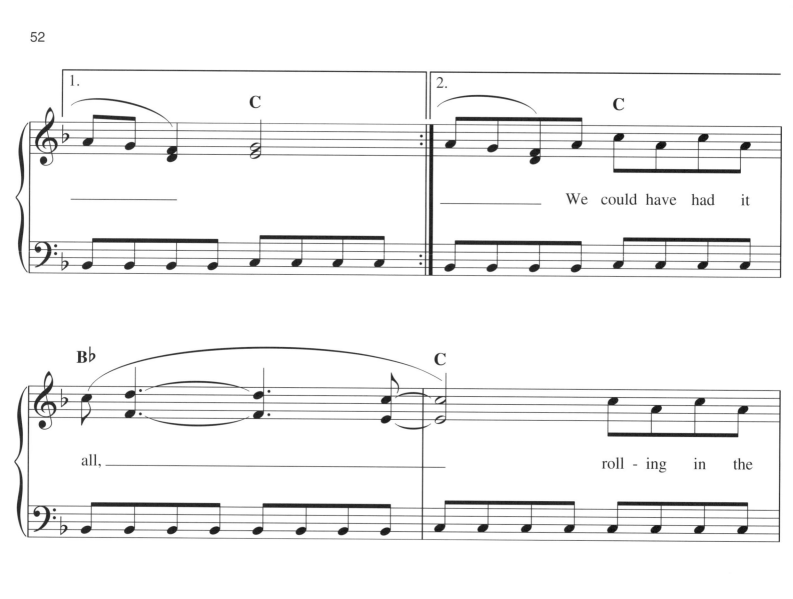

C7   **C**

___ it _____ with a beat - ing...

N.C.

Throw your soul _____ through ev - er - y o - pen door,

count your bless - ings to find what you look for. Turn my sor - row

in - to treas-ured gold. You pay me back in kind and reap just what you sow. ___

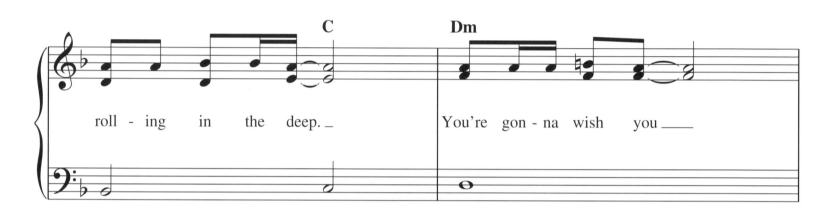

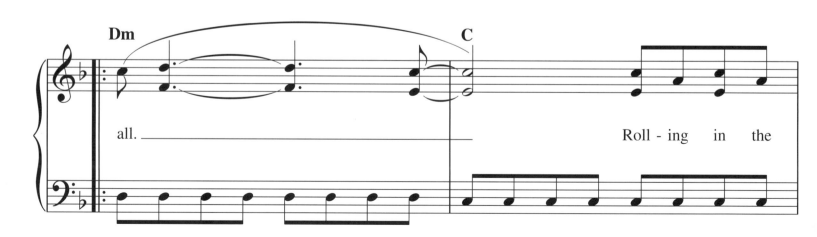

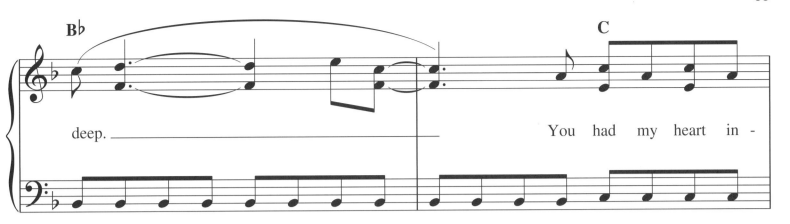

deep. _____ You had my heart in -

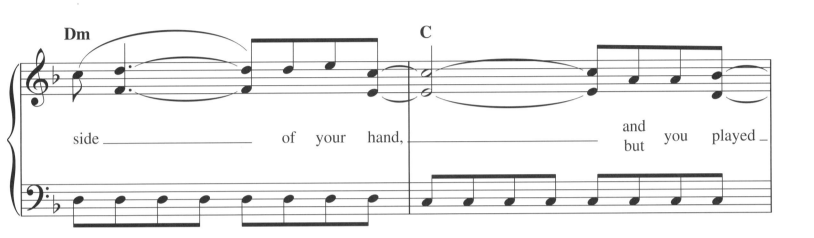

side _____ of your hand, _____ and but you played _

1.

__ it _____ to the beat. _____ We could have had it

2.

__ it, you played _ it, you played __ it, you played _ it to the beat. ___

DANCING QUEEN

Words and Music by BENNY ANDERSSON,
BJÖRN ULVAEUS and STIG ANDERSON

Disco Rock

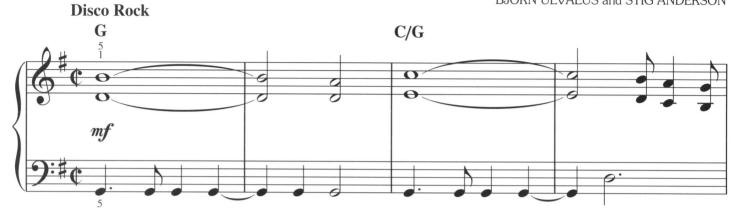

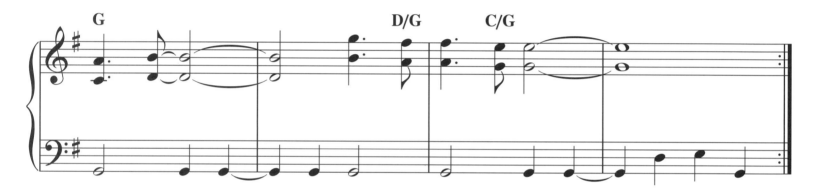

You＿ can dance,＿ you＿ can jive,＿

hav - ing＿ the time of＿ your life.＿

Copyright © 1977 UNIVERSAL/UNION SONGS MUSIKFORLAG AB
Copyright Renewed
All Rights in the United States and Canada Controlled and Administered by UNIVERSAL - SONGS OF POLYGRAM INTERNATIONAL, INC. and EMI GROVE PARK MUSIC, INC.
All Rights Reserved   Used by Permission

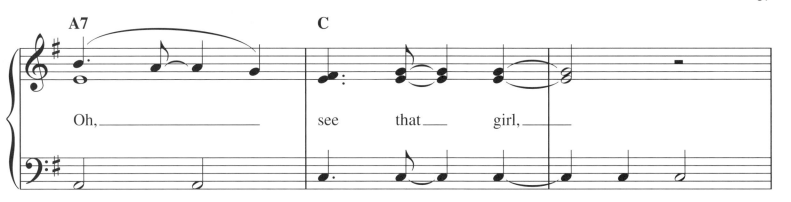

Oh, _____ see that___ girl, ___

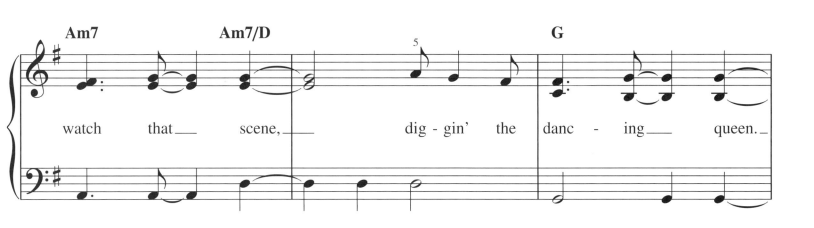

watch that___ scene, ___ dig - gin' the danc - ing___ queen.___

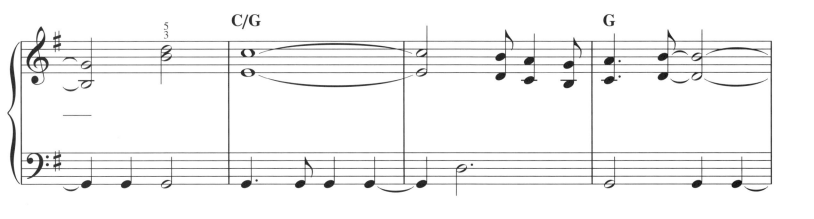

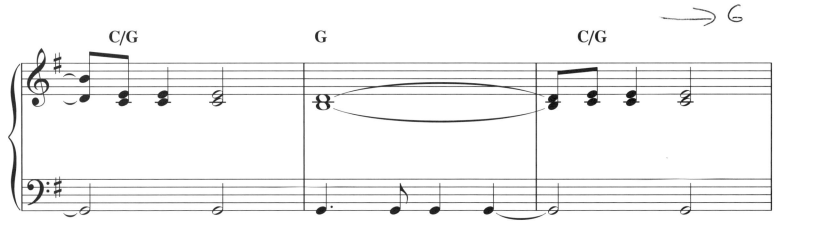

Fri - day night___ and the lights are low,___

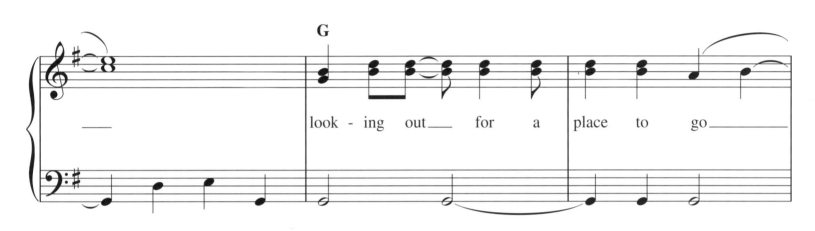

___ look - ing out___ for a place to go___

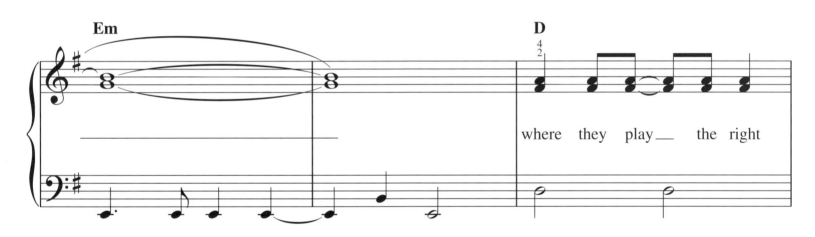

___ where they play___ the right

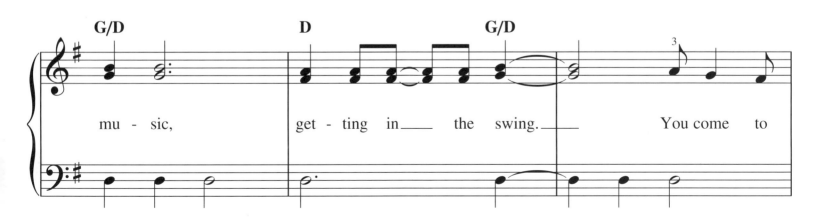

mu - sic, get - ting in___ the swing.___ You come to

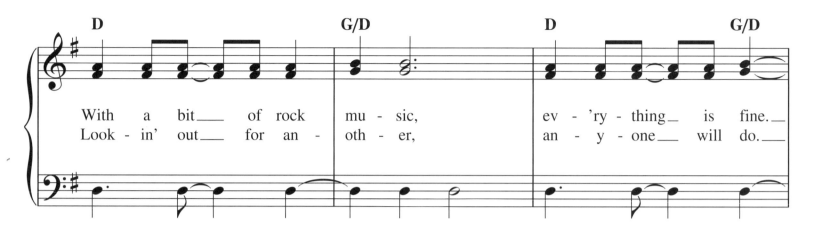

With a bit___ of rock mu – sic, ev – 'ry – thing___ is fine.___
Look - in' out___ for an - oth – er, an – y - one___ will do.___

You're in the mood for a dance.___

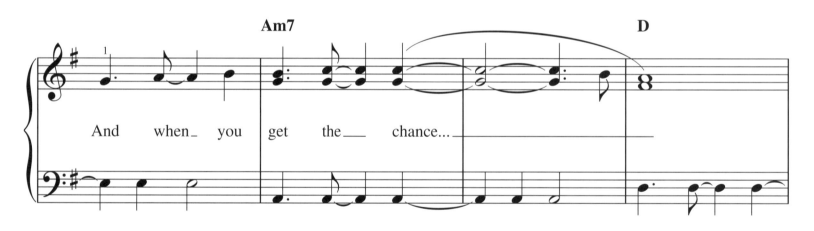

And when___ you get the___ chance...___

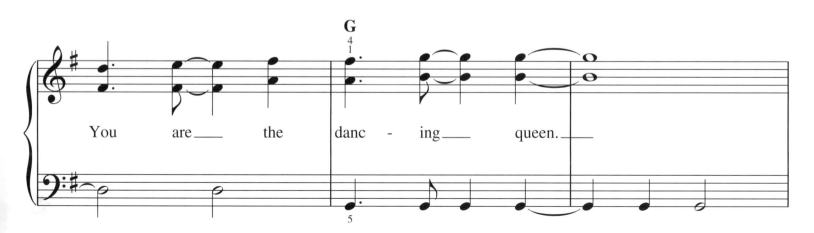

You are___ the danc – ing___ queen.___

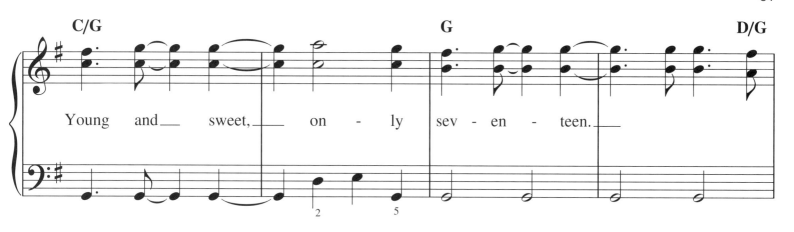

Young and sweet, on - ly sev - en - teen.

Danc - ing queen,

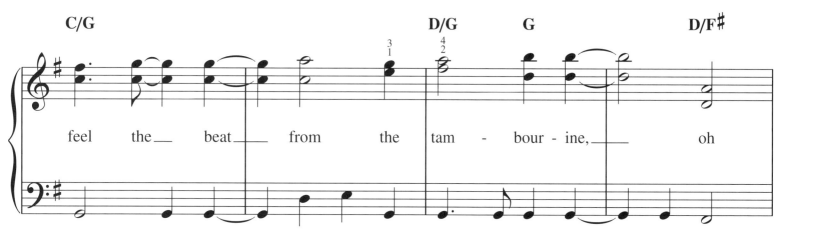

feel the beat from the tam - bour - ine, oh

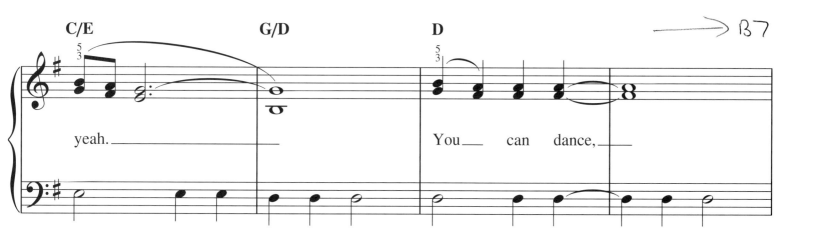

yeah. You can dance,

B7

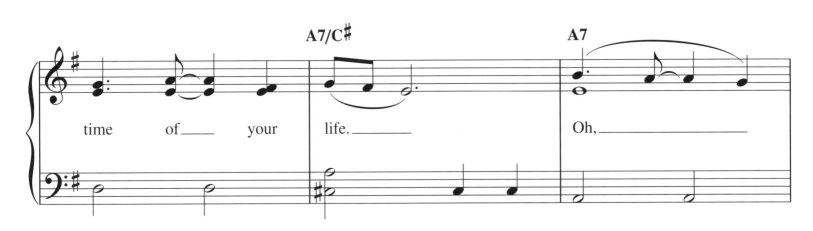

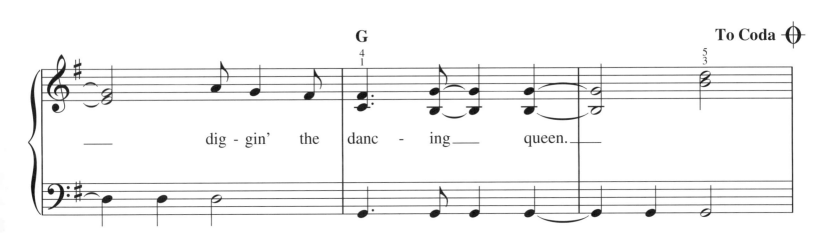

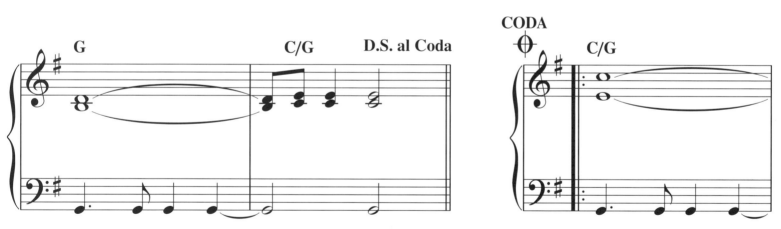

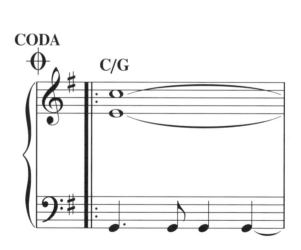

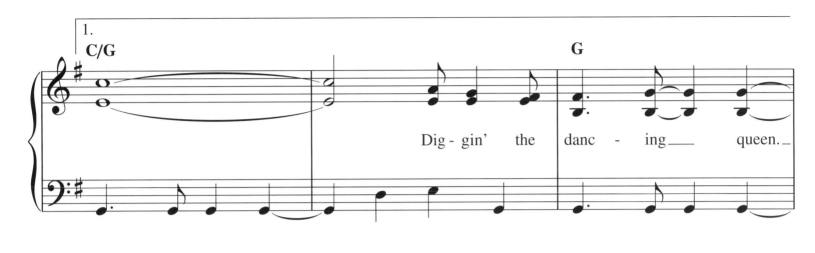

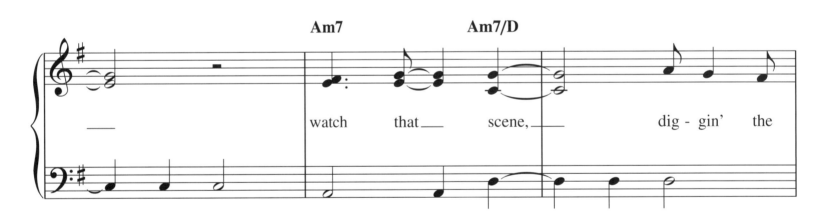

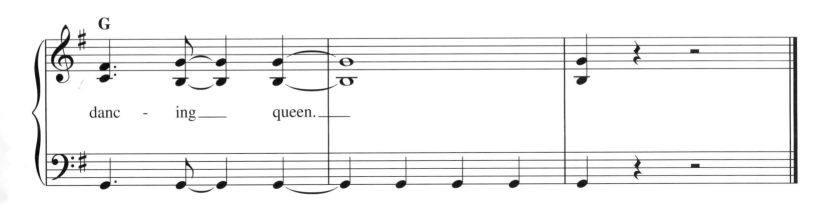

TRY A LITTLE TENDERNESS

Words and Music by HARRY WOODS,
JIMMY CAMPBELL and REG CONNELLY

© 1932 (Renewed) CAMPBELL, CONNELLY & CO., LTD.
All Rights in the United States and Canada Administered by EMI ROBBINS CATALOG INC. (Publishing) and ALFRED MUSIC PUBLISHING CO., INC. (Print)
All Rights Reserved   Used by Permission

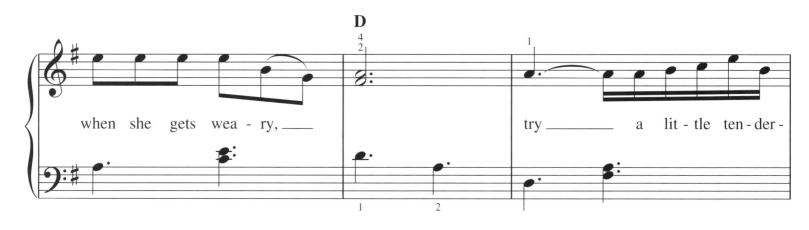

when she gets wea-ry, ____ try _____ a lit-tle ten-der-

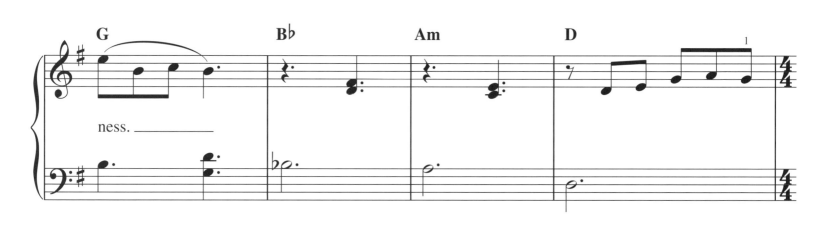

ness. _____

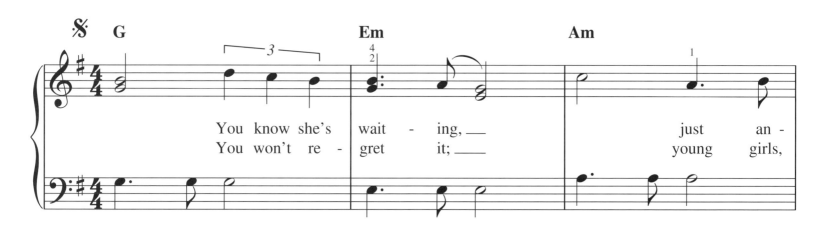

You know she's wait - ing, ___ just an -
You won't re - gret it; ___ young girls,

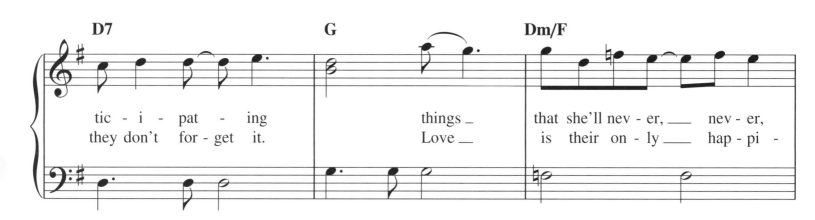

tic - i - pat - ing things __ that she'll nev - er, ___ nev - er,
they don't for - get it. Love __ is their on - ly ___ hap - pi -

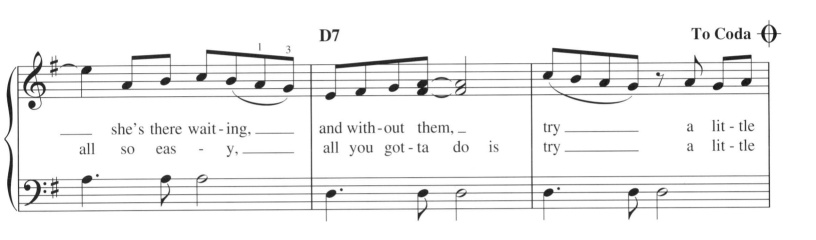

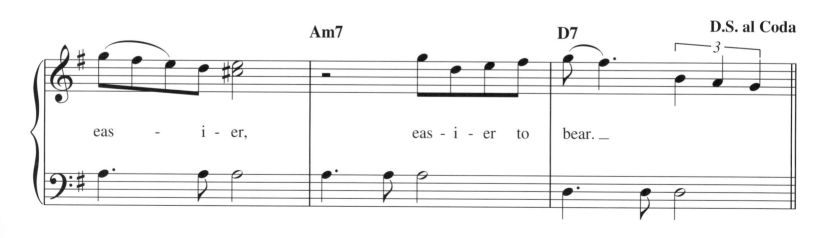

CODA

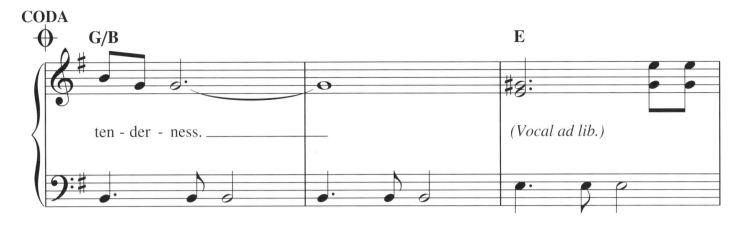

ten - der - ness. _____

(Vocal ad lib.)

rit.

MY MAN
(Mon homme)
from ZIEGFELD FOLLIES

Words by ALBERT WILLEMETZ
and JACQUES CHARLES
English Words by CHANNING POLLOCK
Music by MAURICE YVAIN

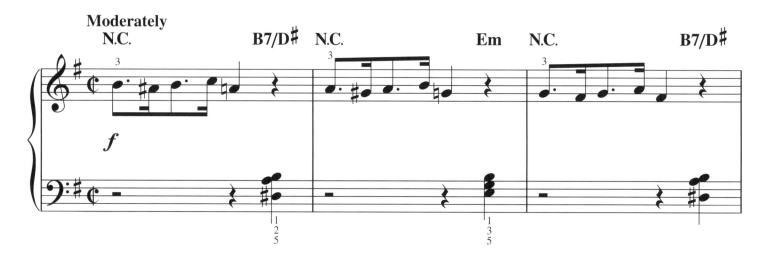

Some-times I say if I | just could get a - way with my
Sur cet - te terr', ma seul' | *joie, mon seul bon - heur c'est mon*

man, ___ | | he'd go straight sure as fate, for it
hom - me | | *J'ai don - né tout c'que j'ai, mon a -*

Copyright © 2011 by HAL LEONARD CORPORATION
All Rights for Canada Administered by EMI FEIST CATALOG INC. (Publishing) and ALFRED PUBLISHING CO., INC. (Print)
International Copyright Secured   All Rights Reserved

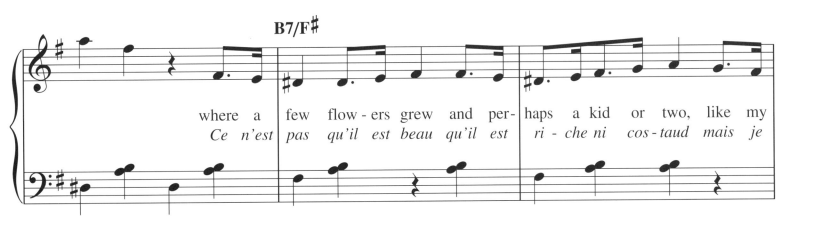

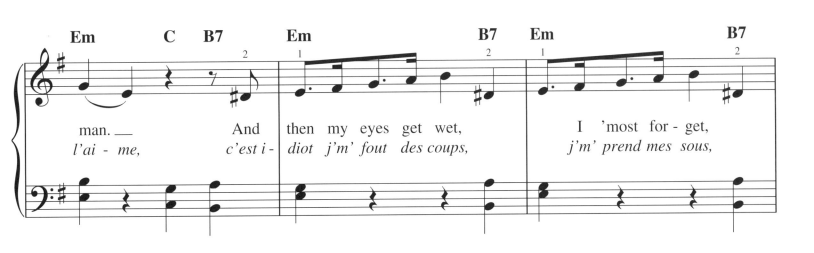

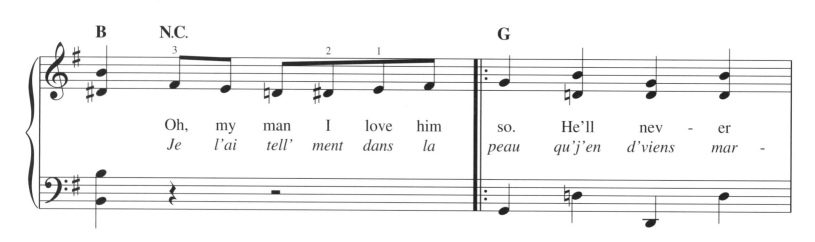

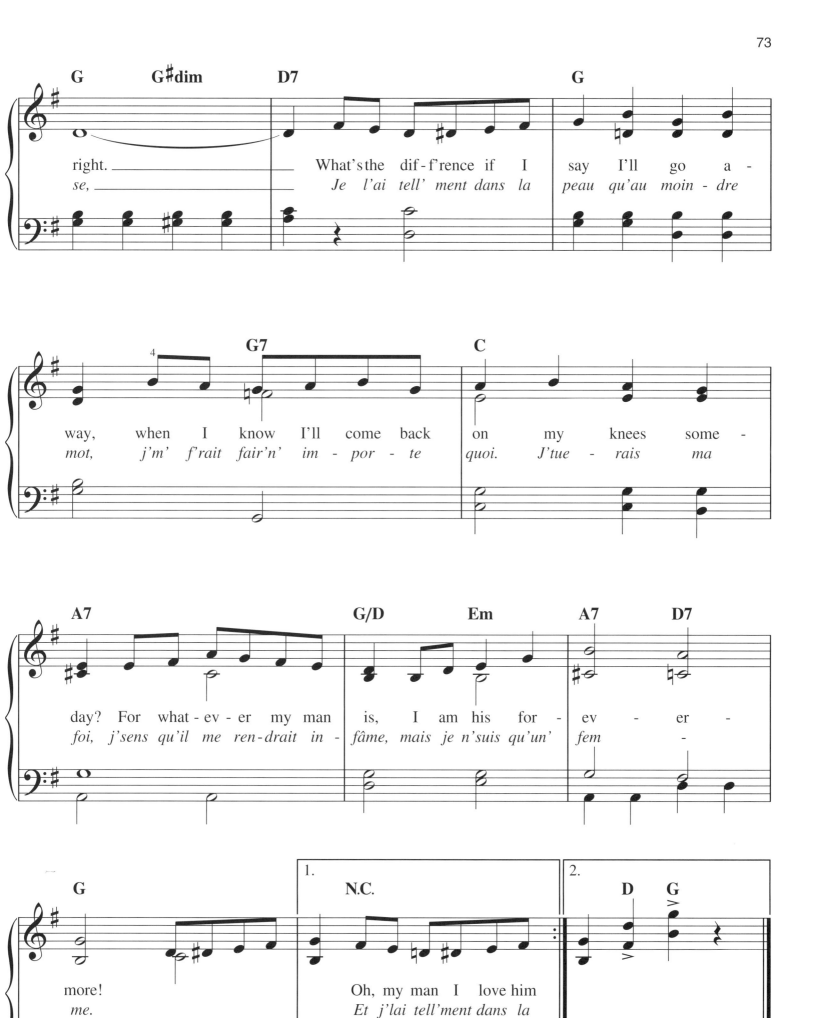

PURE IMAGINATION

from WILLY WONKA AND THE CHOCOLATE FACTORY

Words and Music by LESLIE BRICUSSE
and ANTHONY NEWLEY

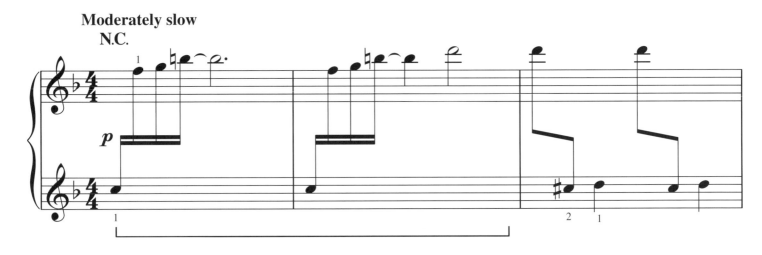

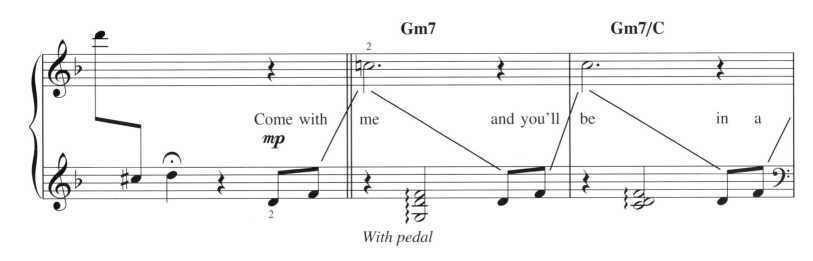

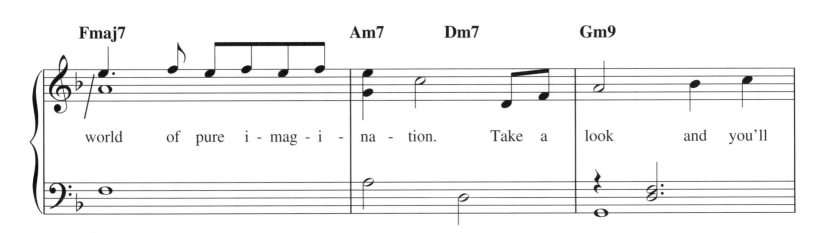

Copyright © 1970, 1971 by Taradam Music, Inc.
Copyright Renewed
International Copyright secured   All Rights Reserved

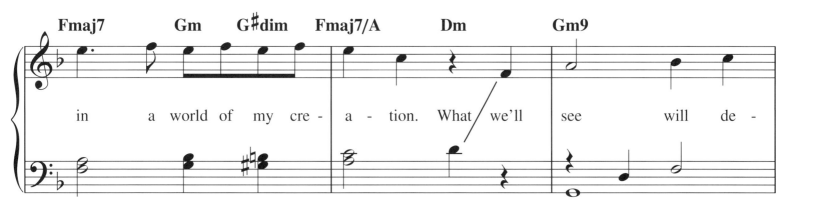

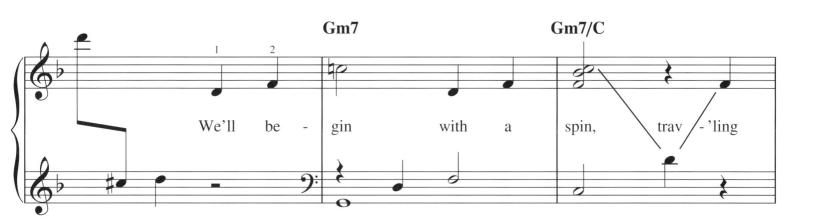

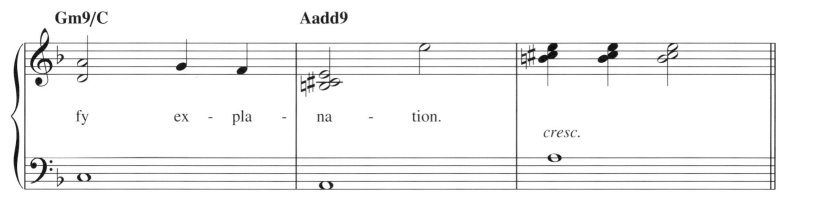

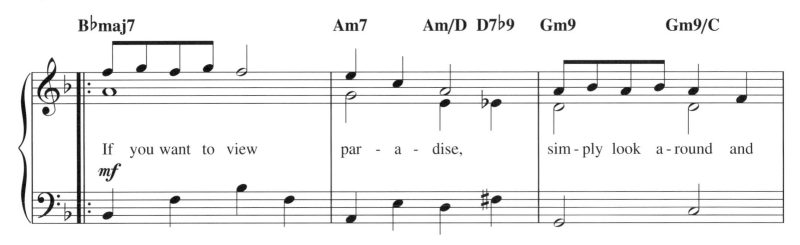

B♭maj7   **Am7**   **Am/D D7♭9**   **Gm9**   **Gm9/C**

If you want to view   par - a - dise,   sim - ply look a - round and

Fmaj9   **Bm7♭5**   **E7**   **Am**

view it.   An - y - thing you want   to,   do it.

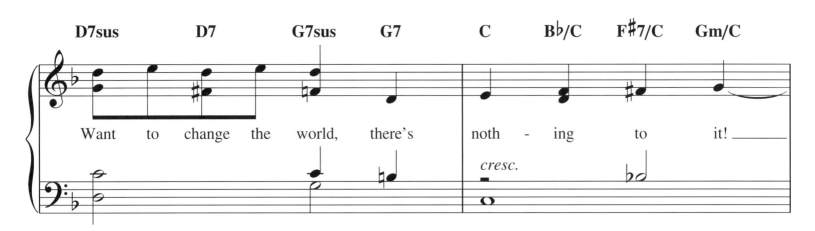

D7sus   **D7**   **G7sus**   **G7**   **C**   **B♭/C**   **F♯7/C**   **Gm/C**

Want   to change the world, there's   noth - ing to it! _____

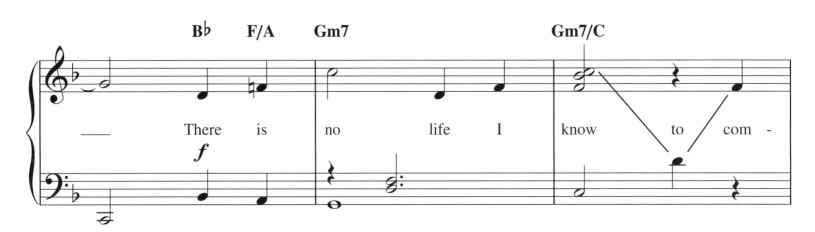

B♭   **F/A**   **Gm7**   **Gm7/C**

_____ There is   no   life I   know   to / com -

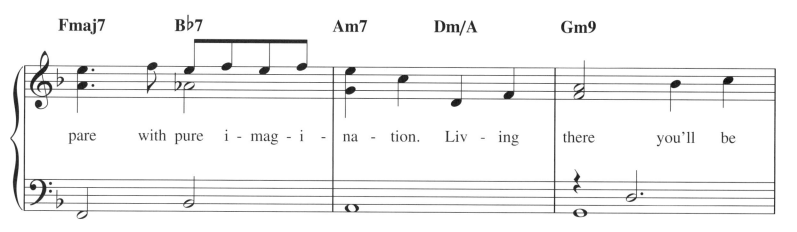

Fmaj7   **B♭7**   **Am7**   **Dm/A**   **Gm9**

pare   with   pure   i - mag - i - na - tion.   Liv - ing   there   you'll   be

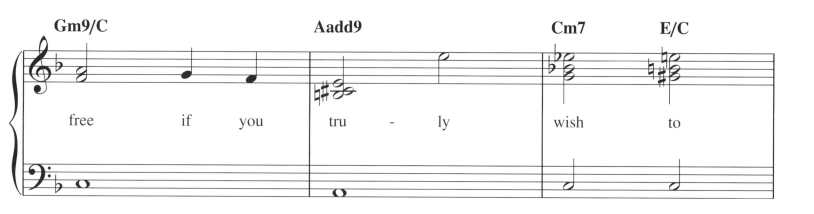

Gm9/C   **Aadd9**   **Cm7**   **E/C**

free   if   you   tru - ly   wish   to

1.   **F**   **F7**   2.   **F**

be.   be.

dim.

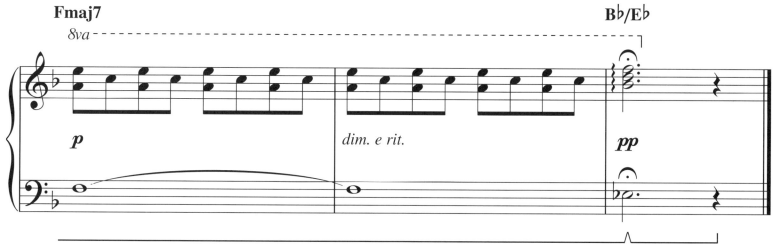

Fmaj7   **B♭/E♭**

8va

p   *dim. e rit.*   *pp*

BELLA NOTTE
(This Is the Night)
from Walt Disney's LADY AND THE TRAMP

Words and Music by PEGGY LEE
and SONNY BURKE

© 1952 Walt Disney Music Company
Copyright Renewed
All Rights Reserved   Used by Permission

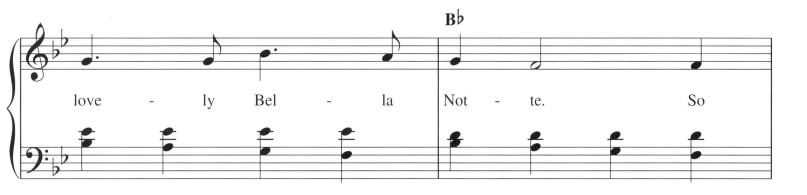

love - ly Bel - la Not - te. So

take this love _____ of your loved one. You'll

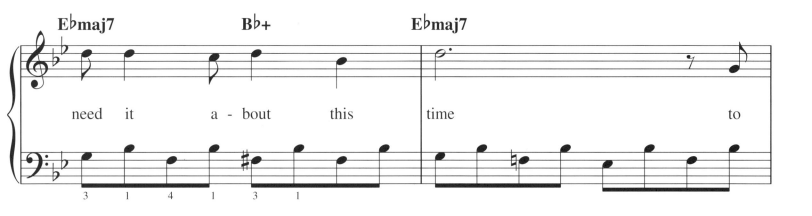

need it a - bout this time to

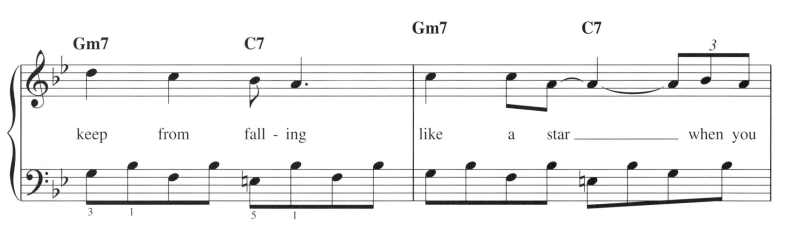

keep from fall - ing like a star _____ when you

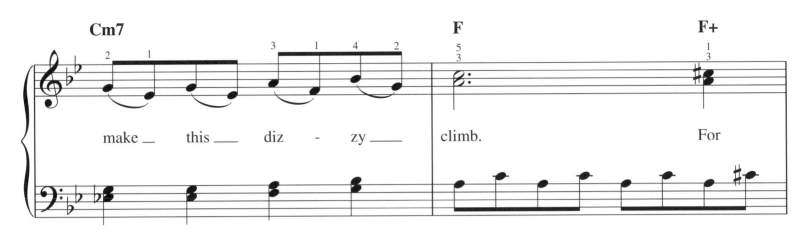

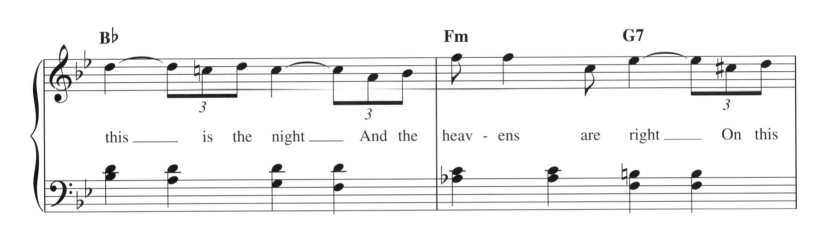

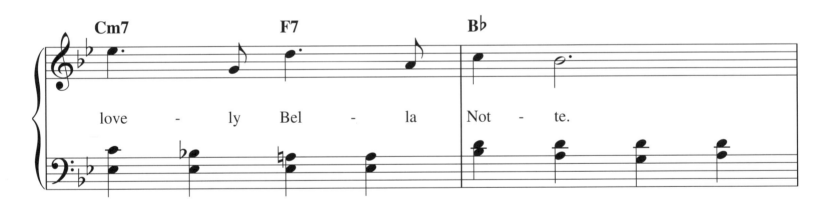

AS LONG AS YOU'RE THERE

Words and Music by ADAM ANDERS,
PEER ASTROM and CLAUDE KELLY

Copyright © 2011 T C F Music Publishing, Inc., Fox Film Music Corp. and Warner-Tamerlane Publishing Corp.
All Rights Reserved   Used by Permission

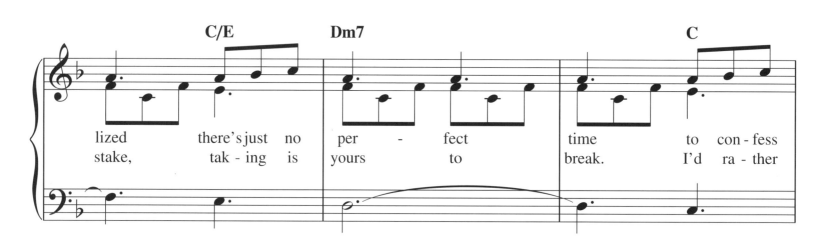

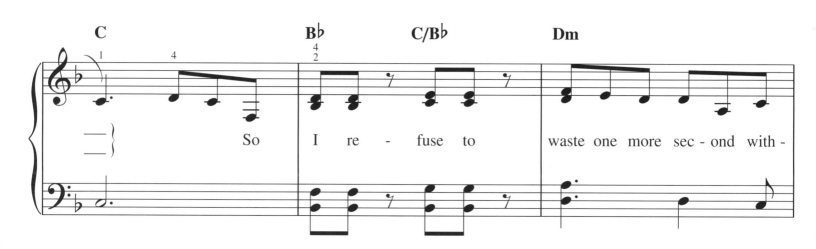

PRETENDING

Words and Music by ADAM ANDERS,
PEER ASTROM and SHELLY PEIKEN

Moderate Ballad

With pedal

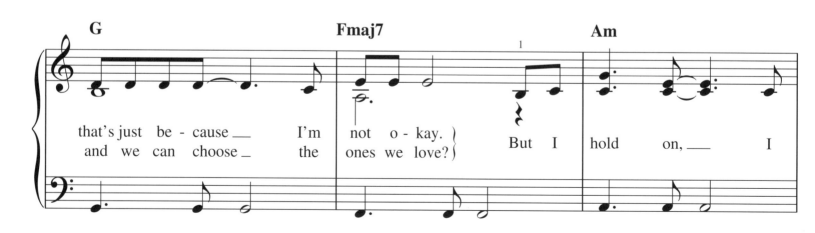

Copyright © 2011 T C F Music Publishing, Inc., Fox Film Music Corp. and ROR Songs
All Rights for ROR Songs Controlled and Administered by Kobalt Music Publishing America, Inc.
All Rights Reserved   Used by Permission

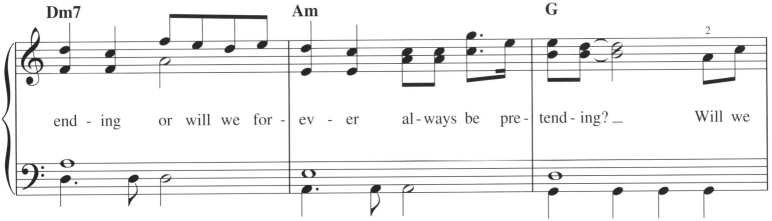

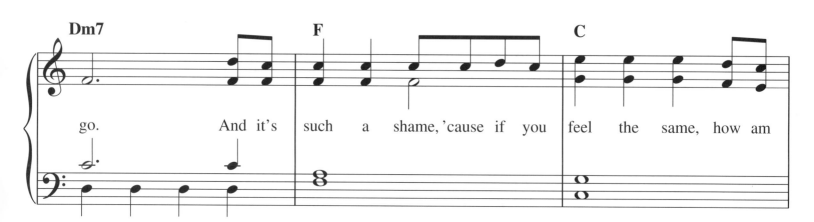

LIGHT UP THE WORLD

Words and Music by ADAM ANDERS,
PEER ASTROM, SAVAN KOTECHA,
MARTIN SANDBERG and JOHAN SCHUSTER

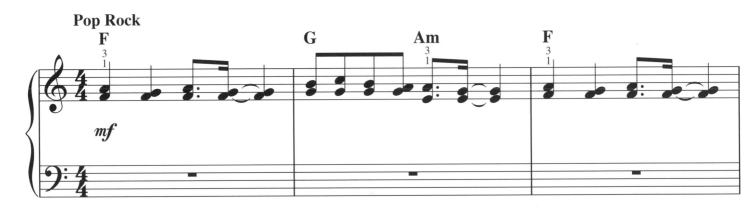

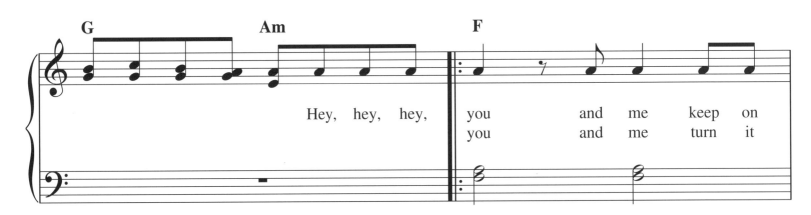

Hey, hey, hey,   you   and me keep on
you   and me turn it

danc-ing in the dark, __ it's been
up ten-thous-and watts, __ tell me

tear-ing me a-part, __ nev-er
why we've got to stop, __ I just

know-ing what we are. __ Hey, hey, hey,   you   and me keep on
want to let it rock. __ Hey, hey, hey,   you   and me keep on

Copyright © 2011 T C F Music Publishing, Inc., Fox Film Music Corp., Mr. Kanani Songs, EMI April Music Inc. and Maratone AB
All Rights for Mr. Kanani Songs Controlled and Administered by EMI April Music Inc.
All Rights for Maratone AB Administered by Kobalt Music Publishing America, Inc.
All Rights Reserved   Used by Permission

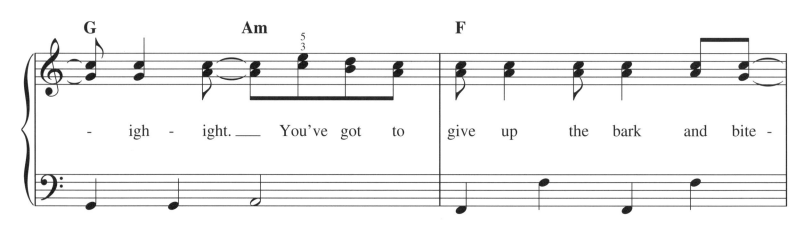

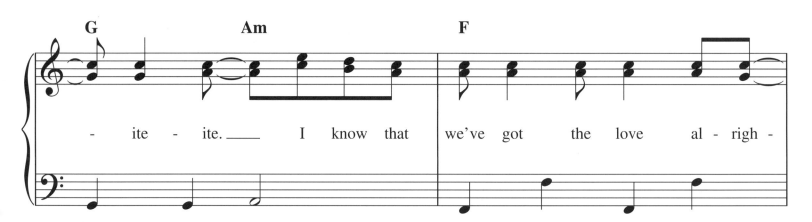

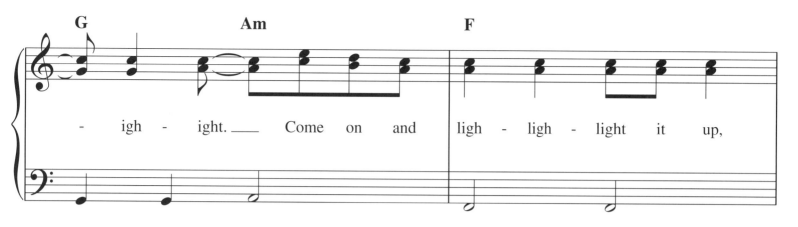

you, you, you, you, you, you, you, you, you. _ Lay it all down, _ I've

got some-thing to say. _ Lay it all down, _ throw your doubt a-way. _ Do or

die now, _ step up to the plate. _ Blow the door wide o-pen like

up, up and a-way. _ Let's

light it up to-night. _ Let's

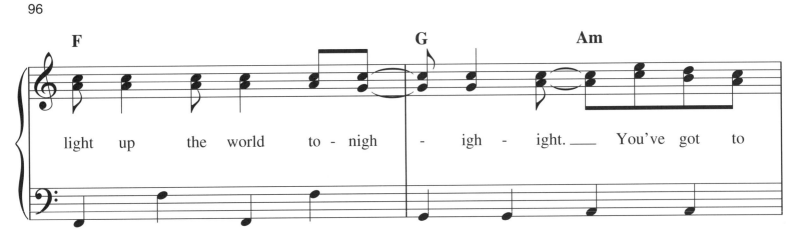

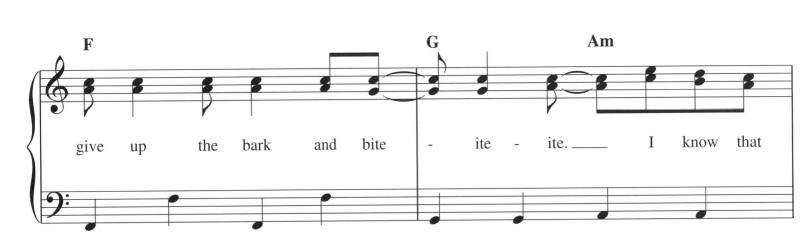

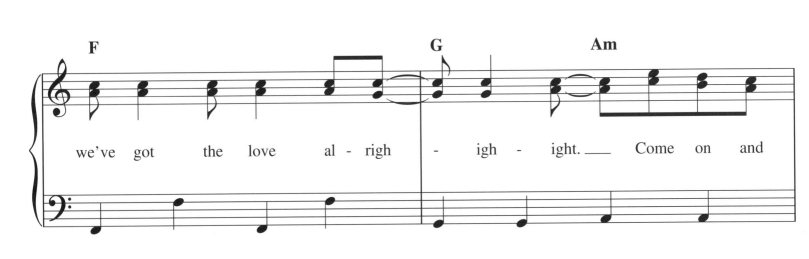